ALL I REALLY NEED TO KNOW I LEARNED IN KINDERGARTEN

ALSO BY ROBERT FULGHUM

It Was on Fire When I Lay Down on It

Maybe (Maybe Not)

Uh-Oh

From Beginning to End

True Love

Words I Wish I Wrote

ALL I REALLY NEED TO KNOW I LEARNED IN KINDERGARTEN

Reconsidered, Revised &
Expanded with
Twenty-Five New Essays

FIFTEENTH ANNIVERSARY EDITION

Robert Fulghum

BALLANTINE BOOKS
NEW YORK

A Ballantine Book
Published by The Random House Publishing Group

Published in the United States by Ballantine Books, an imprint of
The Random House Publishing Group, a division of Random House, Inc.,
New York, and simultaneously in Canada by Random House of
Canada Limited, Toronto.

Originally published in different form by Villard Books,
a division of Random House, Inc., in 1988. A portion of this text appeared
in the *Kansas City Times*.

www.ballantinebooks.com

Text design by Susan Turner

The Cataloging-in-Publication Data for this title is available from the
Library of Congress.

ISBN 978-0-345-46639-6

Manufactured in the United States of America

First Edition: December 1989
First Revised Ballantine Edition: September 2003
First Revised Trade Paperback Edition: May 2004

12 14 16 18 19 17 15 13

TO THE READER FROM THE AUTHOR

THE ORIGINAL EDITION OF THIS BOOK began with words that are important enough to repeat again. If I could give you this book in person I would ask you to keep these things in mind:

What you are about to read was written over many years, a little bit at a time, and often reconsidered and revised. During that time I lived in many places, had many jobs, and traveled widely. The essays and stories were addressed to friends, family, a religious community, students, and myself—with no thought of publication in book form. I think of it as my "stuff"—an account of what goes on in my mind and life.

A part of this—what I learned in kindergarten—was passed around until it took on a life of its own and began to appear on refrigerators and bulletin boards. One day the essay was sent home from school in the knapsack of a child whose mother was a literary agent. The mother wrote to me: Had I written anything else? Well, yes. And one thing led to another in a Wonderland sort of way.

As a kind of "truth in packaging" statement, I tell you here and now that I have changed some names and facts to protect those who are either innocent or crabby or both. I am not an investigative journalist.

Furthermore, I have an official Storyteller's License. A friend made it up and taped it to the wall over my desk. This license gives me permission to use my imagination in rearranging my experience to improve a story, so long as it serves the standard of Truth in the best sense. The truth of poetry and parable do not compete with the truth of science or the courtroom. I trust the reader to know the difference.

Finally, I will not make the usual reservation that "the opinions expressed within are entirely my own." The older I get the more I realize how much I think is a composite of the goods selected from the supermarket shelves of the world of thought. What *is* mine is an *attitude* about what passes through my mind. To expound on that theme, I begin this 15th anniversary edition of this book with a profound admonition found on a bumper sticker:

"DON'T BELIEVE EVERYTHING YOU THINK."

Words on the back bumper of an old blue Ford pickup truck.

Alone in my car in Santa Fe, New Mexico. January. Snowstorm at nightfall. For several blocks all I can clearly see in front of me is this message on the truck's bumper, made urgent by flashing red brake lights. Creep a block. Stop. Flash. Read. Creep another block. Stop. Flash. Re-read:

"DON'T BELIEVE EVERYTHING YOU THINK."

Those words left a permanent afterimage in my mind. They provoke me to recall the dumb or useless or naïve ideas I've held in a lifetime. Ideas I once thought were indelibly tattooed on my brain cells. Ideas I have since discarded when new evidence and further experience forced me to change my mind.

Often, when reading through old journals, I have thought to myself, "I really cannot believe I ever thought that." But I did. I did. And I would have fiercely defended what I thought in the open court of public opinion.

On the other hand:

There *are* things that I *think* that I *do believe*.

These convictions remain steadfast, holding tough and true through all the weather of experience. Some ideas last. They do. The question, of course, is which ones. That's a field-testing issue, isn't it?

The book *All I Really Need to Know I Learned in Kindergarten* has been in print more than fifteen years now. In light of my Santa Fe bumper-sticker experience, I wondered how the ideas in *Kindergarten* would bear up under critical scrutiny. Do I still respect the convictions woven into the stories in that book? Or have I changed my mind? And if I have changed my mind, what to do?

Revising and reissuing a book published fifteen years ago is not commonly done. But why? If the book can be improved and expanded, then it might continue to be useful and meaningful. The *Kindergarten* book represents an attitude—a way of looking at things. Why not look again? So. I looked.

Once I set to work I did more than expected. I removed several stories entirely because they are dated or because I have truly changed my mind or else because I have a new story that better speaks the truth I want to express.

Twenty-five new essays have been added. Most of the old material has been edited or tidied up for the sake of clarity. The order has been changed for the sake of continuity. As it now stands, the book seems like a final form.

Yet—I wonder. How will I feel about this writing fifteen years from now, if indeed I am around to feel at all? If life goes well, I will probably reconsider and revise the book again. I hope so. The reason will remain the same: I will have changed my mind, recognizing that I no longer believe everything I once thought. Or else I will also find then what I have found now: that many of my convictions have not altered and bear repeating. My Storyteller's Creed is an example:

I believe that imagination is stronger than knowledge—
That myth is more potent than history.
That dreams are more powerful than facts—
That hope always triumphs over experience—
That laughter is the only cure for grief.
And I believe that love is stronger than death.

—ROBERT FULGHUM, 2003

ALL I REALLY
NEED TO KNOW
I LEARNED IN
KINDERGARTEN

CREDO

To begin with, did I really learn everything I need to know in kindergarten? Do I still believe that? Here is the original essay, followed by my editorial reaction.

EACH SPRING, FOR MANY YEARS, I have set myself the task of writing a personal statement of belief: a Credo. When I was younger, the statement ran for many pages, trying to cover every base, with no loose ends. It sounded like a Supreme Court brief, as if words could resolve all conflicts about the meaning of existence.

The Credo has grown shorter in recent years—sometimes cynical, sometimes comical, and sometimes bland—but I keep working at it. Recently I set out to get the statement of personal belief down to one page in simple terms, fully understanding the naïve idealism that implied.

The inspiration for brevity came to me at a gasoline station. I managed to fill my old car's tank with super deluxe high-octane go-juice. My old hoopy couldn't handle it and got the willies—kept sputtering out at intersections and belching going downhill. I understood. My mind and my spirit get like that from time to time. Too much high-content information, and I get the existential willies. I keep sputtering out at intersections where life choices must be made and I either know too much or not enough. The examined life is no picnic.

I realized then that I already know most of what's necessary to live a meaningful life—that it isn't all that complicated. I *know it*. And have known it for a long, long time. Living it—well, that's another matter, yes? Here's my Credo:

ALL I REALLY NEED TO KNOW about how to live and what to do and how to be I learned in kindergarten. Wisdom was not at the top of the graduate-school mountain, but there in the sandpile at Sunday School. These are the things I learned:

Share everything.

Play fair.

Don't hit people.

Put things back where you found them.

Clean up your own mess.

Don't take things that aren't yours.

Say you're sorry when you hurt somebody.

Wash your hands before you eat.

Flush.

Warm cookies and cold milk are good for you.

Live a balanced life—learn some and think some and draw and paint and sing and dance and play and work every day some.

Take a nap every afternoon.

When you go out into the world, watch out for traffic, hold hands, and stick together.

Wonder. Remember the little seed in the Styrofoam cup: The

roots go down and the plant goes up and nobody really knows how or why, but we are all like that.

Goldfish and hamsters and white mice and even the little seed in the Styrofoam cup—they all die. So do we.

And then remember the Dick-and-Jane books and the first word you learned—the biggest word of all—LOOK.

Everything you need to know is in there somewhere. The Golden Rule and love and basic sanitation. Ecology and politics and equality and sane living.

Take any one of those items and extrapolate it into sophisticated adult terms and apply it to your family life or your work or your government or your world and it holds true and clear and firm. Think what a better world it would be if we all—the whole world—had cookies and milk about three o'clock every afternoon and then lay down with our blankies for a nap. Or if all governments had as a basic policy to always put things back where they found them and to clean up their own mess.

And it is still true, no matter how old you are—when you go out into the world, it is best to hold hands and stick together.

DEEP KINDERGARTEN

As I WRITE THIS I am sixty-five years old. Not so old, really, but I have been around awhile. Kindergarten is a long way back there. What do I know now?

The Kindergarten Credo is not kid stuff.

It is not *simple*. It is *elemental*.

The essay answers the questions asked sooner or later by every one of us who once stared out a classroom window wondering: Why am I here? Why do I have to go to school?

We are sent to school to be civilized—to be introduced to the essential machinery of human society. Early on in our lives we are sent out of the home into the world. To school. We have no choice in this. Society judges it so important that we be educated that we *must* go. It is the law. And when we get to school we are taught the fundamentals on which civilization rests. These are first explained in language a small child understands.

For example, it would do no good to tell a six-year-old that "Studies have shown that human society cannot function without an equitable distribution of the resources of the earth." While this statement is profoundly and painfully true, a child cannot comprehend this vocabulary. So a child is told that there are twenty children and five balls to play with; likewise four easels, three sets of blocks, two guinea pigs, and one bathroom. To be fair, we must share.

Likewise a six-year-old will not understand that "By and large it has been demonstrated that violence is counterproductive to the constructive interaction of persons and societies." True. But a child can better understand that the rule out in the world and in the school is the same: *Don't hit people*. Bad things happen. The child must understand this rule is connected to the first rule: People won't share or play fair if you hit them.

It's hard to explain the cost and consequences of environmental pollution and destruction to a six year old. But we are paying a desperate price even now because adults did not heed the instructions of kindergarten: Clean up your own mess; put things back where you found them; don't take what's not yours.

"The history of society is more defined by its understanding of disease than its formulation of philosophy and political theory." True. Basic sanitation. Keeping excrement off our hands as well as out of our minds is important. But it's enough to teach a child to use the toilet, flush, and wash his hands regularly.

And so on. From the first day we are told in words we can handle what has come to be prized as the foundation of community and culture. Though the teacher may call these first lessons "simple rules," they are in fact the distillation of all the hard-won, field-tested working standards of the human enterprise.

Once we are told about these things, we soon discover we are taking a lab course. We are going to be asked to try and practice these precepts every day. Knowledge is meaningful only if it is reflected in action. The human race has found out the hard way that we are what we do, not just what we think. This is true for kids and adults—for schoolrooms and nations.

I am sometimes amazed at what we did not fully grasp in kindergarten. In the years I was a parish minister I was always taken aback when someone came to me and said. "I've just come from the doctor and he told me I have a only a limited time to live."

I was tempted to shout, "*What?* You didn't know? You had to pay a doctor to tell you—at your age? Where were you the week in kindergarten when you got the little cup with the cotton and water and seed? Life happened—remember? A plant grew up and the roots grew down. A miracle. And then a few days later the plant was dead. DEAD. Life is short. Were you asleep that week or home sick or what?"

I never said all that. But I thought it. And it's true. The idea was for us to have the whole picture right from the beginning. Life-and-death. Lifedeath. One event. One short event. Don't forget.

There's another thing not everyone figures out right away: It's almost impossible to go through life all alone. We need to find our support group—family, friends, companion, therapy gatherings, team, church or whatever. The kindergarten admonition applies as long as we live: "When you go out into the world, hold hands and stick together." It's dangerous out there—lonely, too. Everyone needs someone. Some assembly is always required.

What we learn in kindergarten comes up again and again in our lives as long as we live. In far more complex, polysyllabic forms, to be sure. In lectures, encyclopedias, bibles, company rules, courts of law, sermons, and handbooks. Life will examine us continually to see if we have understood and have practiced what we were taught that first year of school.

Across the course of our lives we will wrestle with questions of right and wrong, good and bad, truth and lies. Again and again and yet again, we will come around to that place where we came in—to that room where the elemental notions about humanity were handed to us with great care when we were very young.

Of course it wasn't literally all you really needed to know. Certainly not. But if you didn't get this basic stuff to begin with, you and society will pay a heavy price for your failure. If you did learn it and do practice it, then all the rest of what you needed to know has a lasting foundation.

There, now.

The Kindergarten Credo amplified, but unchanged.

That's what I believe and know and trust at age sixty-five.

THE REST OF THE STORY

"AND SO THEN WHAT HAPPENED?"

An urgent question out of the bedtime darkness, asked by my children, when they and I were young. Just when I thought I had slam-dunked a story ending—just when I was certain the children were safely in the arms of the sandman—a small, sleepy voice would plead, "So, then what happened?" And no matter what I replied, the plea went on, "Please, please, Daddy—tell the rest of the story."

In cranky desperation, I would resort to apocalypse: "Suddenly a comet hit the earth and blew everything to pieces."

Silence. "What happened to the pieces?"

"It doesn't matter. Everybody died a horrible death, especially all the little children who were not asleep." I also tried, "The father sold all the children who would not go to sleep to a passing gypsy who ground them into sausage meat. The first children to be ground up were those who would not stop asking questions."

Go ahead, shame me. But it worked. Most of the time. On reflection, I suspect such gory endings were what they really liked most. Perhaps it was a scheme to see just how far I would go—to see how crazed their father really was.

Now I am dealing with grandchildren who have the same restless minds. I am wilier now than I used to be. To the inevitable request for more, I reply, "Only your father knows the rest of the story. Ask him to finish it when you get home."

The children are right to ask, of course. As long as life exists, something always happens next. There are always consequences—always sequels.

Anticipating future bedtime insistence, I've been reviewing my repertoire of stories. And I must say I wonder myself what did happen next?

After the la-di-da with Little Red Riding Hood, did the word get passed among wolves to stay away from smarty-pants little girls who are magnets for trouble? And how come Red's bedridden grandma was living way off in the woods alone instead of in a retirement community or a nursing home?

How about Alice? Could she find her way back into Wonderland in middle age when she could really have used a little excitement in her life? Of course not. Whenever she approached a looking glass, she touched up her makeup.

After the blind men examined the elephant and came back to the king with their paradoxical impressions, did they pool their contradictions and re-examine the elephant? Don't bet on it. They'd rather have their heads cut off than give up their prejudices. The wise man who had grabbed the tail insisted, "An elephant is like a rope. Everybody else is wrong." The wise man in the middle declared, "No, an elephant is like four tree trunks. Everybody else is wrong." And the wise man who encountered the trunk insisted the elephant was a hose—period.

Could Snow White really live happily ever after when the prince knew she had been living with seven little men for some time? No way. He'd always bring it up when they had a family fight. "What did you really *do* with all those little men?"

And Cinderella couldn't have lived too happily with a prince who couldn't recognize her unless she was wearing the right slippers.

Remember the story of the emperor's new clothes? The emperor had been duped by a tailor into believing that the clothes he made were so magnificent that only the pure of heart could wear them. When the emperor strutted his stuff in the non-existent clothes, a kid said what everybody could plainly see: "The emperor is stark naked." What happened to that kid? He was hauled off home and sent to bed without his supper for being a big mouth and making trouble for his family.

The kid had always been told: "Be truthful, speak your mind, be true to yourself and have the courage of your convictions." But the kid found out the hard way what the real rules were: "Don't make waves, keep your mouth shut, cover your butt, don't be a hero and mind your own business." Whistle-blowers, like girls who marry a prince, do not live happily ever after. The kid wrestled with this reality as long as he lived.

OK, call me old and cynical. Go on, treat me like the parents treated the kid who called the emperor naked. Tell me I should be like the blind men and not rearrange my stories in the face of further information.

Maybe I know too much and have lived too long. Better I leave truth out of bedtime stories or pass the buck to their parents. It's too soon to tell them the world is not always nice or fair. Children will find out the rest of the story on their own. Soon enough, there will be sleepless nights when "What will happen next?" will not be a plot inquiry but the entreaty of prayer.

SPIDERS

THIS IS MY NEIGHBOR. Nice lady. Coming out her front door, on her way to work and in her "looking good" mode. She's locking the door now and picking up her daily luggage: purse, lunch bag, gym bag for aerobics, and the garbage bucket to take out. She turns, sees me, gives me the big, smiling Hello, takes three steps across her front porch. And goes "AAAAAAAA-GGGGGGGGGGHHHHHHHHHH!!!!" *(That's a direct quote.)* At about the level of a fire engine at full cry.

Spider web! She has walked full force into a spider web. And the pressing question, of course: Just where is the spider *now*?

She flings her baggage in all directions. And at the same time does a high-kick, jitterbug sort of dance—like a mating stork in crazed heat. Clutches at her face and hair and goes "AAAAAAA-GGGGGGGGHHHHHHHHHH!!!!!" at a new level of intensity. Tries opening the front door without unlocking it. Tries again. Breaks key in the lock. Runs around the house headed for the back door. Doppler effect of

"A A A A A G G G H H H H a a g g h . . ."

Now a different view of this scene. Here is the spider. Rather ordinary, medium gray, middle-aged lady spider. She's been up since before dawn working on her web, and all is well. Nice day, no wind, dew point just right to keep things sticky. She's out checking the moorings and thinking about the little gnats she'd like to have for breakfast. Feeling good. Ready for action. All of a sudden all hell breaks loose—earthquake, tornado, volcano. The web is torn loose and is wrapped around a frenzied moving haystack, and a huge piece of raw-but-painted meat is making a sound the spider has never heard: "AAAAAAAGGGGGGGGGHHHHHHH!!!!!"

It's too big to wrap up and eat later, and it's moving too much to hold down.

Jump for it? Hang on and hope? Dig in?

Human being. The spider has caught a human being. And the pressing question is, of course: Where is it going and what will it do when it gets there?

The neighbor lady thinks the spider is about the size of a lobster and has big rubber lips and poisonous fangs. The neighbor lady will probably strip to the skin and take a full shower and shampoo just to make sure it's gone—and then put on a whole new outfit to make certain she is not inhabited.

The spider? Well, if she survives all this, she will *really* have something to talk about—the one that got away that was THIS BIG. "And you should have seen the JAWS on the thing!"

Spiders. Amazing creatures. Been around maybe 350 million years, so they can cope with about anything. Lots of them, too—sixty or seventy thousand per suburban acre. Yes. It's the web thing that I envy. Imagine what it would be like if people were equipped like spiders. If we had this little six-nozzled aperture right at the base of our spine and we could make yards of something like glass fiber with it. Wrapping packages would be a cinch!

Mountain climbing would never be the same. Think of the Olympic events. And mating and child rearing would take on new dimensions. Well, you take it from there. It boggles the mind. Cleaning up human-sized webs would be a mess, on the other hand.

All this reminds me of a song I know. And you know, too. And your parents and your children, they know. About the itsy-bitsy spider. Went up the waterspout. Down came the rain and washed the spider out. Out came the sun and dried up all the rain. And the itsy-bitsy spider went up the spout again. You probably know the motions, too.

What's the deal here? Why do we all know that song? Why do we keep passing it on to our kids? Especially when it puts spiders in such a favorable light? Nobody goes "AAAAAAA-GGGGGGGGGHHHHHHHHH!!!!!" when they sing it. Maybe because it puts the life adventure in such clear and simple terms. The small creature is alive and looks for adventure. Here's the drainpipe—a long tunnel going up toward some light. The spider doesn't even think about it—just goes. Disaster befalls it—rain, flood, powerful forces. And the spider is knocked down and out beyond where it started. Does the spider say, "To hell with that"? No. Sun comes out—clears things up—dries off the spider. And the small creature goes over to the drainpipe and looks up and thinks it *really* wants to know what is up there. It's a little wiser now—checks the sky first, looks for better toeholds, says a spider prayer, and heads up through mystery toward the light and wherever.

Living things have been doing just that for a long, long time. Through every kind of disaster and setback and catastrophe. We are survivors. And we teach our kids about that. And maybe spiders tell their kids about it, too, in their spider way.

So the neighbor lady will survive and be a little wiser coming out the door on her way to work. And the spider, if it lives, will do likewise. And if not, well, there are lots more spiders, and the word gets around. Especially when the word is "AAAAAAA GGGGGGGGGHHHHHHHHHH!!!!"

———————

Often, when speaking in public, I begin by saying I will silently sing. As a clue to what's going on in my mind, I explain, I will make some motions with my hands. I ask the audience to help me out by doing the same thing when they understand what's going on. It's the spider song, of course. I have great memories of rooms full of people silently singing the itsy-bitsy spider, while doing the motions, and grinning. They always grin. They always applaud themselves at the end.

Did you know that you can sing the words to the itsy bitsy spider to the tune of the "Ode to Joy" portion of Beethoven's Ninth symphony? With some minor adjustments it works. You might call the combination the fight song of the human race. I once got a thousand people to do it, motions and all.

Both pieces of music are about the same thing: the capacity of life to triumph over adversity—about perseverance in adventure, for spiders and people.

PUDDLES

I T'S MAY IN CENTRAL PARK in New York City. An afternoon shower followed by seductive spring sunshine lures busy people off sidewalks and onto park benches. At 80th Street and Fifth Avenue there's a path into the park, on which the rain has left an obstacle course of puddles.

A small child, kitted out in full raingear, runs splashing through a puddle, "YAAAAAAAAHHH." His mother, likewise rainproofed, runs after him, shouting, "NO. NO. NO." Catching his hand, she pulls him back onto dry land and barks sternly: "NO PUDDLES, Jacob. I told you: NO PUDDLES."

The child strains outward and away from her like a guy wire from a tent in a windstorm. He whines. The mother pulls him further away down the path. The child upshifts into a wail. The mother tries to pick him up. The child goes limp and screams. It's a standoff. A child-in-the-checkout-line-at-the-supermarket deal. And this kid is a black-belt screamer: "WHOOOAAAOOOYAAAA." The mother is embarrassed. People are staring. (*What did she do to him?*)

A well-dressed middle-aged man observes from a nearby bench.

He's wearing polished black leather wing-tipped shoes. Between him and the mother-and-child hoo-ha is a large puddle. The man stands. Walks deliberately into the puddle, wing-tips and all. Grins. Shouts, "HEY-HEY-HEY." Mother and child look up. The kid goes silent, stands still.

This scene is too good to be true. How can I stay out of this? I get up off my bench and walk into the puddle to stand beside the grinning man. I'm wearing serious leather sandals and socks. I grin at the man and the mom and the kid. A fashionably dressed young woman takes off her shoes and joins us, as does her dog.

The kid laughs, lets go of his mom's hand, and marches into the puddle.

All eyes are on the mom.

Now at center stage, the mom wears an expression of pained pleasure. She's caught again in a parenthood paradox. On the one hand, the child must learn to mind. But, then, what harm can a puddle do if the kid is wearing rain boots? She doesn't want him to get sick. But of course everybody knows you catch colds from germs on other peoples' hands, not from puddles. It's hard to back down when you've said "NO!" But it's not wrong to change your mind. She doesn't want her child to follow the example of strangers. But all these three people have done is to stand in the puddle and grin at her. How can so much be at stake over such a small event? What's a good mother to do?

Being a parent always involves some hypocrisy. If she were a kid, she'd be in the puddle now. She walked in puddles when she was a child and came to no harm. Her mom probably shouted "NO PUDDLES" at her, too. Does parenthood always mean being driven by the autopilot of the past?

All this races through the mom's mind in nanoseconds.

The waders and watchers are waiting. She can't stand there forever.

The mom smiles. Laughs. Walks into the puddle. Her audience applauds.

The waders shake her hand, shake each other's hands and go their ways.

The child has a pleased-but-stupefied look on his face.

Adults are weird. He will not understand how weird until he is one.

So, you may ask, did this really happen?

Well, yes and no. The day and the park and the puddle were real. The small cast assembled in this little arena was there. And the inclinations we all had were right and true. But, in fact, the mother pulled the kid off down the path, still barking "NO PUDDLES" at him, and leaving the rest of us grumpily minding our own business. Still, it *might* have happened. It *should* have happened. Puddles are there as a test about staying young as long as you can. All the adults there that day failed the test.

How I hated walking away thinking, as I have so many times in my life, that next time or when I have time or when circumstances are just right I will do what my heart says to do. Sometimes acting foolish and being wise are the same.

Later that afternoon I went back to do what I knew I should have done.

Too late. Too late.

Mother and child and nice people and puddle and opportunity had gone.

HAIHO LAMA

Elias Schwartz repairs shoes. He is short and round and bald and single and middle-aged and Jewish. "An old-fashioned cobbler," says he, nothing more, nothing less. I happen to be convinced that he is really the 145th reincarnation of the Haiho Lama.

See, the Haiho Lama died in 1937, and the monks of the Saskya monastery have been searching for forty years for his reincarnation without success. *The New York Times* carried the story last summer. The article noted that the Lama would be recognized by the fact that he went around saying and doing wise things in small, mysterious ways, and that he would be doing the will of God without understanding why. A guy like that would be worth looking for, all right.

I found him. Through some unimaginable error in the cosmic switching yards, the Haiho Lama has been reincarnated as Elias Schwartz. I have no doubts about it.

My first clue came when I took my old loafers in for total renewal. The works. Elias Schwartz examined them with intense care. With regret in his voice he pronounced them not worthy of repair. I accepted the unwelcome judgment. Then he took my shoes, disappeared into the back of the shop, and I waited and wondered. He returned with my shoes in a stapled brown bag. For carrying, I thought.

When I opened the bag at home that evening, I found two gifts and a note. In each shoe, a chocolate-chip cookie wrapped in waxed paper. And these words in the note: "Anything not worth doing is worth not doing well. Think about it. Elias Schwartz."

The Haiho Lama strikes again.

And the monks will have to go on looking.

Because I'll never tell—we need all the Lamas here we can get.

ANGELS

"**A**RE YOUR STORIES TRUE? Are the people real?"
The simple answer is Yes. The more complicated answer is that I am a storyteller, not an investigative journalist. A good story can be improved by adding necessary facts—spice to the stew. A dash of hyperbole may be used to encourage laughter. And sometimes I combine two very similar good stories into one better story—sacrificing what is true for the sake of Truth. Often it's necessary to change names and certain identifying details to protect the privacy of the individuals about whom I write. Not everybody wants to be well known.

A case in point is the Haiho Lama.

The story is true. But, from the beginning, the shoemaker was adamant about not being identified. He felt it was not right to get credit for simply doing what everybody ought to do in the first place. "Please don't use my name or tell people where my shop is," he asked. So I made up a name: Elias Schwartz. It was just as well. The shoemaker's real name was too improbable to be credible: Eli Angel.

Mr. Angel is dead now, and I feel free to correct the facts and tell you the rest of the story.

Eli Angel was an Orthodox Sephardic Jew born on the island of Rhodes. Though his formal education was limited, those who knew him considered him a very learned man. He could hold his own in Greek, Spanish, French, Hebrew, and English. He knew history and philosophy and theology. A generous man, he was active in helping other immigrants settle into their adopted country. In his neighborhood in Seattle he was revered for his many small acts of perceptive kindness, for believing that whatever good a man does comes back to him. When he died, the synagogue was filled to overflowing. They called him a *tzaddik*—a righteous man, worthy of respect.

By coincidence, my wife knew Eli's wife. My wife, the epitome of medical discretion, had never told me that she was Mrs. Angels's physician. After Eli's death, Mrs. Angel was feeling pretty bad and came to see my wife. She missed her beloved husband. She wished more people had known him. My wife told her the story of the Haiho Lama from the *Kindergarten* book, and explained that millions of people knew about her husband—they just didn't know his real name. His acts of kindness had come back around to comfort his wife.

Doing good things without expectation of reward was Eli's specialty—way beyond putting cookies in shoes he wouldn't repair.

The Jews have a word for such deeds—*mitzvoh*.

Mrs. Angel died recently. And now I can tell you even more.

When Eli met Rachael, it was love at first sight. He proposed after knowing her two days. She turned him down. Why? Because she had cancer; she had been told she could not have children and would not live long. He insisted. He would love her until the end, whenever it came. With love as a shield against impending doom, they married. Love produced four children. And love kept them together into old age. Mrs. Angel was as good at *mitzvoh* as her husband—a conspirator in doing good deeds without getting caught at it.

I know all this because I recently spent time talking with Angels. Eli's son is a third-generation cobbler, running his father's shop up on Capitol Hill in Seattle. People in the neighborhood speak of Raymond as they once spoke of his father—a real *mensch*—a worthy man. I watched him engage customers with patience and attention. Another *mitzvoh* specialist, I thought to myself.

I spoke with Raymond's sisters and his daughter, and saw the family scrapbooks. Eli Angel and his dear wife, Rachael, were talked about as if they were still around—still taking care of their corner of the world. I went away reminded that not all people are no damned good and the world is not going completely to hell. I went away admonished and blessed.

The evangelist, Billy Graham, says angels are real, we just can't see them.

Wrong.

I know where the real Angels are. I have seen them with my own eyes.

Some Angels I know can fix your soles. And mend your soul at the same time.

HIDE AND SEEK

IN THE EARLY DRY DARK of an October Saturday evening, the neighborhood children are playing hide-and-seek. How long since I played hide-and-seek? Fifty years; maybe more. I remember how. I could become part of the game in a moment, if invited. Adults don't play hide-and-seek. Not for fun, anyway. Too bad.

Did you have a kid in your neighborhood who always hid so good, nobody could find him? We did. After a while we would give up on him and go off, leaving him to rot wherever he was. Sooner or later he would show up, all mad because we didn't keep looking for him. And we would get mad back because he wasn't playing the game the way it was supposed to be played. There's *hiding* and there's *finding*, we'd say. And he'd say it was hide-and-seek, not hide-and-GIVE-UP, and we'd all yell about who made the rules and who cared about who, anyway, and how we wouldn't play with him anymore if he didn't get it straight and who needed him anyhow, and things like that. Hide-and-seek-and-yell. No matter what, though, the next time he would hide too good again. He's probably still hidden somewhere, for all I know.

As I write this, the neighborhood game goes on, and there is a kid under a pile of leaves in the yard just under my window. He has been there a long time now, and everybody else is found and they are about to give up on him over at the base. I considered going out to the base and telling them where he is hiding. And I thought about setting the leaves on fire to drive him out. Finally, I just yelled, "GET FOUND, KID!" out the window. And scared him so bad he probably wet his pants and started crying and ran home to tell his mother. It's real hard to know how to be helpful sometimes.

A man I know found out last year he had terminal cancer. He was a doctor. And knew about dying, and he didn't want to make his family and friends suffer through that with him. So he kept his secret. And died. Everybody said how brave he was to bear his suffering in silence and not tell everybody, and so on and so forth. But privately his family and friends said how angry they were that he didn't need them, didn't trust their strength. And it hurt that he didn't say good-bye.

He hid too well.

Getting found would have kept him in the game. Hide-and-seek, grown-up style. Wanting to hide. Needing to be sought. Confused about being found. "I don't want anyone to know." "What will people think?" "I don't want to bother anyone."

Better than hide-and-seek, I like the game called Sardines. In Sardines the person who is It goes and hides, and everybody goes looking for him. When you find him, you get in with him and hide there with him. Pretty soon everybody is hiding together, all stacked in a small space like puppies in a pile. And pretty soon somebody giggles and somebody laughs and everybody gets found.

Medieval theologians even described God in hide-and-seek terms, calling him *Deus Absconditus*. But me, I think old God is a Sardine player. And will be found the same way everybody gets found in Sardines—by the sound of laughter of those heaped together at the end.

"Olly-olly-oxen-free." The kids out in the street are hollering the cry that says, "Come on in, wherever you are. It's a new game." And so say I. To all those who have hid too good:

Get found, kid! Olly-olly-oxen-free.

CHICKEN-FRIED STEAK

THE WINDING DOWN OF SUMMER puts me in a philosophical mood. I am thinking about the deep, very private needs of people. Needs that when met give us a great sense of well-being. We don't like to talk about these for fear that people will not understand. But to increase our level of intimacy, I will tell you about one of my needs: chicken-fried steak.

You take a piece of stringy beef, pound hell out of it with a kitchen sledge, dip the meat in egg and flour, drop it in a skillet with bacon drippings, and fry it up crisp. There you have it: chicken-fried steak.

Next you take the meat out of the pan, throw in some flour and milk and salt and pepper, and you got serious gravy. On the plate with the steak you lay peas and mashed potatoes, and then dump on the gravy. Some cornbread and butter and a quart of cold whole milk on the side are necessary. Then you take knife and fork in hand, hunker down close to the trough, lift your eyes heavenward in praise of the wonders of the Lord, and don't stop until you've mopped up the last trace of gravy with the last piece of cornbread.

Disgusting, you say. Absolutely disgusting. Sure. Like a lot of good eating, this began as a way to disguise a sorry piece of old meat so you can't see or taste it. And you probably eat something that stands for home and happiness that I wouldn't approach without a Geiger counter and a bomb squad. It's okay. You eat yours and I'll eat mine.

Now everybody has some minor secret yearnings in life. And I've kind of been keeping my eye out for the ultimate chicken-fried-steak experience. You have to look in truck stops and little country towns off the freeway. Little temples of the holy meal out there in the underbrush, reached by blue highways or dirt roads.

If you're interested, one summer's search produced these results:

One Star to the Torres Bar and Grill in Weiser, Idaho—free toothpicks, too.

Two Stars to the Farewell Bend Cafe in Farewell Bend, Oregon—with special praise for a side of "Graveyard Stew," which is milk toast, and that's another story.

Two Stars to the Blue Bucket in Umatilla, Oregon—free mints afterward.

Three Stars to the Roostertail Truck Stop on Sixth Avenue South in Seattle—the waitress used to drive a truck in Alabama. She knows all about chicken-fried steak.

Five stars and a bouquet to Maud Owens's Cafe in Payette, Idaho, where the chicken-fried steak hangs over the edge of the plate and is accompanied by parsley, a spiced peach, two dill pickles, and a fried egg. *And* free toothpicks *AND* free mints. *And* a map of Payette under the plate. The manager shook my hand when I left. The waitress gave me a kiss on the cheek. I left her a two-dollar tip. I don't think anybody had ever eaten the whole thing before. I could still taste it three days later.

The Rolling Stones are famous for their phrase about how you can't always get what you want but sometimes you can get what you need. Well, I'm here to tell you that sometimes you can get what you want *and* what you need at the same time, with free toothpicks and mints, and a kiss for topping!

I wrote that gloria to chicken-fried steak a long, long time ago. I have not changed my mind one bit. After the story appeared in print I got a call from a traveling salesman who had checked out the cafes I mentioned in the story. He had an update. Some are still cooking, but one of the best had been closed by the health authorities. Seems they found dirt in the cream gravy. The salesman said he was told that the cafe regulars figured now they knew the cafe's secret ingredient.

He nominated Mom's Café in Salina, Utah. I went. I ate. A four-star winner.

To guarantee that a blue-ribbon version of chicken-fried steak will always be available close by, I made a special arrangement with my favorite Seattle cafe. (The Shanty—on the waterfront at 350 Elliot Avenue West. No dress code, no valet parking, and no violence. A sign on the wall says, "All perverts must be on a leash.")

On the dinner menu now is the Captain Kindergarten Blue Plate Special. It's gourmet chicken-fried steak. An aged, choice, lean, New York strip steak that's been butterflied, pounded, dipped in fresh egg wash, peppered, dredged with flour and bread crumbs (from sourdough bread), and fried light golden brown (ninety seconds on a side) on a hot grill that has been greased with a little butter and a touch of bacon drippings. The steak covers the whole platter it's served on. Everything that goes with it comes in little dishes on the side: rolls, soup or salad, mashed or French fried potatoes, corn or green beans, a pitcher of cream gravy, and fresh seasonal fruit or custard pie. Endless iced tea or coffee. A toothpick, a mint, great conversation, and a hug from the waitress. (Worth a generous tip.)

I once talked them into cooking chicken-fried bacon for me.

Oh sure, I know if you eat this way you'll die.

So? If you don't eat this way you're still going to die.

Why not die happy?

CHARLES BOYER

THIS IS KIND OF PERSONAL. It may get a little syrupy, so watch out. It started as a note to my wife. And then I thought that since some of you might have husbands or wives and might feel the same way, I'd pass it along. I don't own this story, anyway. Charles Boyer does.

Remember Charles Boyer? Suave, dapper, handsome, graceful. Lover of the most famous and beautiful ladies of the silver screen. That was on camera and in the fan magazines. In real life it was different.

There was only one woman. For forty-four years. His wife, Patricia. Friends said it was a lifelong love affair. Soul mates. They were no less lovers and friends and companions after forty-four years than after the first year.

Then Patricia developed cancer of the liver. And though the doctors told Charles, he could not bear to tell her. And so he sat by her bedside to provide hope and cheer. Day and night for six months. He could not change the inevitable. Nobody could. And Patricia died in his arms. Two days later Charles Boyer was also dead. By his own hand. He said he did not want to live without her.

He said, "Her love was life to me."

This was no movie. As I said, it's the real story—Charles Boyer's story.

It is not for me to pass judgment on how he handled his grief. But it is for me to say that I am touched and comforted in a strange way. Touched by the depth of love behind the apparent sham of Hollywood love life. Comforted to know that a man and woman can love each other that much that long.

I don't know how I would handle my grief in similar circumstances. I pray I shall never have to stand in his shoes. *(Here comes the personal part—no apologies.)* But there are moments when I look across the room—amid the daily ordinariness of life—and see the person I call my wife and friend and companion. And I understand why Charles Boyer did what he did. It really is possible to love someone that much. I know. I'm certain of it.

RACCOONS

THIS IS ABOUT LOVE and a house I once lived in. An elderly lake-side cottage built at the end of the road at the end of the nine-teenth century. A summer place for a family who traveled by horse and buggy out from Seattle through deep woods and over steep hills on logging trails. It was wild there, then, and it is wild there still.

The house sat off the ground on bricks, surrounded by thickets of blackberry bushes and morning-glory vines bent on a struggle to the death. And even though it is only minutes, now, from downtown, squirrels, rabbits, feral pussycats, and "things" I never saw but only heard had long established squatters' rights on the property.

And raccoons. We had raccoons. Big ones. Several.

For reasons known only to God and the hormones of rac-coons, they chose to mate underneath my house. Every spring. And for reasons known only to God and the hormones of rac-coons, they chose to mate underneath my house at three A.M.

Until you have experienced raccoons mating underneath your bedroom at three in the morning, you have missed one of life's more sensational moments. It is an uncommon event, to say the least. If you've ever heard cats fighting in the night, you have a clue. Mag-

34

nify the volume and the intensity by ten. It's not what you'd call a sensual and erotic sound. More like a three-alarm fire is what it is.

I remember the first time it happened. Since conditions were not really conducive to sleep, I got up. When I say I got up, I mean *I GOT UP*. About three feet. Straight up. Covers and all.

When I had recovered my aplomb and adjusted to the new adrenaline level, I got a flashlight and went outside and peered up under the house. This lady raccoon and her suitor were squared off in a corner, fangs bared, covered with mud and blood, and not looking very sexy at all.

Neither my presence nor the beam of light could override what drove them on. With snarls and barks and screams, the passionate encounter raged on. While I watched, the matter was finally consummated and resolved. They had no shame. What had to be done was done. And they wandered off, in a kind of glazy-eyed stupor, to groom themselves for whatever might come next in the life of a raccoon.

I sat there in the rain, my light still shining into the trysting chamber. And I pondered. Why is it that love and life so often have to be carried forth with so much pain and strain and mess? I ask you, why is that?

I was thinking of my own sweet wife in the bed right above me, and our own noises of conflict mixed with affection. I wondered what the raccoons must conclude from the sounds a husband and wife make at night—the ones that sound like "If-you-really-loved-me-you-would-not-keep-making-such-a-mess-in-the-bathroom," followed by "OH, YEAH? WELL, LET ME TELL YOU A FEW THINGS . . ."

Why isn't love easy?

I don't know.

And the raccoons don't say.

LARRY WALTERS

OW LET ME TELL YOU about Larry Walters, my hero. Walters is a truck driver, thirty-three years old. He is sitting in his lawn chair in his backyard, wishing he could fly. For as long as he could remember, he wanted to go up. To be able to just rise right up in the air and see for a long way. The time, money, education, and opportunity to be a pilot were not his. Hang gliding was too dangerous, and any good place for gliding was too far away. So he spent a lot of summer afternoons sitting in his backyard in his ordinary old aluminum lawn chair—the kind with the webbing and rivets. Just like the one you've got in your backyard.

The next chapter in this story is carried by the newspapers and television. There's old Larry Walters up in the air over Los Angeles. Flying at last. Really getting UP there. Still sitting in his aluminum lawn chair, but it's hooked on to forty-five helium-filled surplus weather balloons. Larry has a parachute on, a CB radio, a six-pack of beer, some peanut butter and jelly sandwiches, and a BB gun to pop some of the balloons to come down. And instead of being just a couple of hundred feet over his neighborhood, he shot up eleven thousand feet, right through the approach corridor to the Los Angeles International Airport.

Walters is a taciturn man. When asked by the press why he did it, he said: "You can't just sit there." When asked if he was scared, he answered: "Wonderfully so." When asked if he would do it again, he said: "Nope." And asked if he was glad that he did it, he grinned from ear to ear and said: "Oh, yes."

The human race sits in its chair. On the one hand is the message that says there's nothing left to do. And on the other hand, people like Larry Walters are busy tying balloons to their chairs, directed by dreams and imagination to do their thing.

The human race sits in its chair. On the one hand is the message that the human situation is hopeless. Meanwhile, people like Larry Walters soar upward knowing anything is possible, sending back the message from eleven thousand feet: "I did it, I really did it. I'm FLYING!"

It's the spirit here that counts. The time may be long, the vehicle may be strange or unexpected. But if the dream is held close to the heart, and imagination is applied to what there is close at hand, everything is still possible.

But wait! Some cynic from the edge of the crowd insists that human beings still *can't really* fly. Not like birds, anyway. True. But somewhere in some little garage, some maniac with a gleam in his eye is scarfing vitamins and mineral supplements, and practicing flapping his arms faster and faster and faster.

THE TRUTH ABOUT LARRY WALTERS

THE GREAT BALLOON CHAIR RIDE happened in 1982. I first wrote about it that year. And I told Larry's story for years afterward. Truly, he was a hero to me. As it turned out, some of my facts about Larry and his ride were wrong. And there is a sequel to the story—an ending that is not an ending.

First of all, Larry did not go up to 11,000 feet.

Actually, it was *16,000 feet*. More than three miles up. We know that from the pilots of the TWA and Delta jetliners who found Larry in their airspace. *Sixteen thousand feet. In a lawn chair over Los Angeles.*

He did have a seat belt. But he was so excited he forgot to buckle it. The rest of his gear included an altimeter, a compass, flashlight and extra batteries, beef jerky, a California road map, and a first aid kit. This was no spur-of-the-moment event. Larry was prepared.

His glasses fell off on ascent, and he dropped the BB gun he was going to use to pop balloons to control his altitude. He crash-landed into power lines and blacked out a neighborhood.

Larry's amazing feat did not go unpunished. The FAA cited

him for, among other things, "operating a civil aircraft for which there is not currently in effect an airworthiness certificate" and for being in an airport space and not contacting the control tower. Fine: $1,500.

For a while Larry was famous. *The New York Times*. The *Tonight Show*. Letterman. All that. If you want to know all the details, go to *www.markbarry.com* on the Internet. Mr. Barry is the authority on Larry Walters. He has gathered photographs of the launching site, Larry in the air, and the crash site.

Mr. Barry has even located the actual lawn chair, which Larry had given to a neighborhood kid. How I would like to have that chair to sit in. But it's on its way to the Smithsonian. Besides, Larry would say I should get my own chair. And get my own balloons. And fly.

There is, as I suggested, an end to the Larry Walters story that is not an end.

Ten years after his flight—on October 6, 1993—Larry Walters went hiking in the Angeles National Forest alone. He shot himself. In the heart. And died.

Why? Why? We don't know why. Nobody saw this coming. Larry left no word.

I guess the depth of his despair matched the height of his imagination.

Larry's photograph is on my wall. He's way, way, up there.

And now he's Up There somewhere—forever.

His tombstone says:

LARRY WALTERS
April 19, 1949—October 6, 1993
Lawn Chair Pilot
Beloved.

BALLOON LAUNCH

THE FOURTH DAY OF THE MONTH of June 1783—more than two hundred years ago. The market square of the French village of Annonay, not far from Paris. On a raised platform, a smoky bonfire fed by wet straw and old wool rags. Tethered above, straining at its lines, a huge taffeta bag—a balloon—thirty-three feet in diameter.

In the presence of a "respectable assembly and a great many other people," and accompanied by great cheering, the *machine de l'aerostat* was cut from its moorings and set free to rise majestically into the noontide sky. Six thousand feet into the air it went, and came to earth several miles away in a field, where it was attacked by pitchfork-waving peasants and torn to pieces as an instrument of evil. The first public ascent of a balloon, the first step in the history of human flight.

Old Ben Franklin was there, in France as the agent of the new American states. He of the key and the kite and the lightning and the bifocals and the printing press. When a bystander asked what possible good this balloon thing could be, Franklin made the memorable retort: *"Eh, a quoi bon l'enfant qui vient de naître?"* ("What good is a newborn baby?") A man of such curiosity and imagination could provide an answer to his own question, and in his journal he wrote: "This balloon will open the skies to mankind." The peasants, too, were not far from wrong. It was also a harbinger of great evil for Annonay, which would one day be leveled by bombs falling from the sky. But I am getting ahead of myself.

Some months before that June day, Joseph-Michel Montgolfier sat one evening staring into his fireplace, watching sparks and smoke rise up the chimney from the evening fire. His imagination rose with the smoke. If smoke floated into the sky, why not capture it and put it in a bag and see if the bag would rise, perhaps carrying something or someone with it?

In his mid-forties, the son of a prosperous paper maker, a believer in the great church that was Science in the eighteenth century, a brilliant and impatient man with time on his hands was Monsieur Montgolfier. And so, with his younger, more methodical brother, Etienne, and the resources of their father's factory, he set to work. With paper bags, then silken ones, and finally taffeta coated with resins. And *voila!* came a day when from the gardens at Versailles a balloon carrying a sheep, a rooster, and a duck went aloft. All survived, proving that there were no poisonous gases in the sky, as some had feared.

The most enthusiastic supporter of the brothers Montgolfier was a young chemist, Jean-François Pilatre de Rozier. He didn't want to make balloons; he wanted to go up in one. The Montgolfiers' interest was in scientific experimentation. They were older, wiser groundlings. Pilatre wanted to fly. He was full of the adventure of youth. And so, that fall, November 21, 1783, Jean-François Pilatre de Rozier got his wish. In the garden of the royal palace at La Muette, in the Bois de Boulogne, at 1:54 P.M., in a magnificent balloon seven stories high, painted with signs of the zodiac and the king's monogram. Up, up, and away he went—higher than treetops and church steeples—coming down beyond the Seine, five miles away.

Joseph-Michel and Etienne Montgolfier lived long and productive scientific lives. They died in their beds, safe on the ground. Two years after his historic flight, trying to cross the English Channel west to east in a balloon, the young Jean-François Pilatre de Rozier plummeted from the sky in flames to his death. But his great-great grandson was later to become one of the first airplane pilots in France.

Well, what's all this about, anyway? It's about the power (and the price) of imagination. "Imagination is more important than information." Einstein said that, and he should know.

It's also a story about how people of imagination stand on one another's shoulders. From the ground to the balloon to the man in the balloon to the man on the moon. Yes. Some of us are ground crew—holding lines, building fires, dreaming dreams, letting go, and watching the upward flight. Others of us are bound for the sky and the far edges of things. That's in the story, too.

These things come to mind at the time of year when children graduate to the next stage of things. From high school, from college, from the nest of the parent. What shall we give them on these occasions? Imagination, a shove out and up, a blessing.

"Come over here," we say. "To the edge," we say. "Let us show you something," we say. "We are afraid," they say. "It's very exciting," they say. "Come to the edge," we say. "Use your imagination."

And they come. And they look. And we push. And they fly. We to stay and die in our beds. They to go and to die howsoever, yet inspiring those who come after them to find their own edge. And fly.

These things come to mind, too, in the middle years of my

own life. I, too, intend to live a long and useful life, and die safe in my bed on the ground. But the anniversary of that little event in the village of Annonay just happens to be my birthday. And on its bicentennial I went up in a balloon, from a field near the small Skagit Valley village of La Conner. Up, up, and away.

It's *never* too late to fly!

LAUNDRY

FOR A LONG TIME I was in charge of the laundry at our house. I liked my work. In an odd way it gave me a feeling of involvement with the rest of the family. It also gave me time alone in the back room, without the rest of the family, which was also nice, sometimes.

I like sorting the clothes—lights, darks, and in-betweens. I like setting the dials—hot, cold, rinse, time, and heat. These are choices I can understand and make with decisive skill. I still haven't figured out the new stereo, but washers and dryers I can handle. The bell dings—you pull out the warm, fluffy clothes, take them to the dining-room table, sort and fold them into neat piles. I especially like it when there's lots of static electricity and you can hang socks all over your body and they will stick there.

When I'm finished, I have a sense of accomplishment. A sense of competence. I am good at doing the laundry. At *least* that. And it's a religious experience, you know. Water, earth, fire—polarities of wet and dry, hot and cold, dirty and clean. The great cycles—round and round—beginning and end—Alpha and Omega, amen.

I am in touch with the GREAT SOMETHING-OR-OTHER. For a moment, at least, life is tidy and has meaning. But then, again . . .

The washing machine died last week. Guess I overloaded it with towels. And the load got all lumped up on one side during the spin cycle. So it did this incredible herky-jerky lurching dance across the floor and blew itself up. I thought it was coming for me. One minute it was a living thing in the throes of a seizure, and the next minute a cold white box full of partially digested towels with froth around its mouth, because I guess I must have fed it too much soap, too. Five minutes later the dryer expired. Like a couple of elderly folks in a nursing home who follow one another quickly in death, so closely are they entwined.

It was Saturday afternoon, and all the towels in the house were wet, and all my shorts and socks were wet, and now what? Knowing full well that if you want one of those repair guys you have to stay home for thirty-six hours straight and have your banker standing by with a certified check or else they won't set foot on your property, and I haven't got time for that. So it's the laundromat over at the mall.

Now I haven't spent a Saturday night in the laundromat since I was in college. What you miss by not going to laundromats anymore are things like seeing other people's clothes and overhearing conversations you'd never hear anywhere else. I watched an old lady sort out a lot of sexy black underwear and wondered if it was hers or not. And heard a college kid explain to a friend how to get puke off a suede jacket.

Sitting there waiting, I contemplated the detergent box. I use Cheer. I like the idea of a happy wash. Sitting there late at night, leaning against the dryer for warmth, eating a little cheese and crackers and drinking a little white wine out of the thermos (*I came prepared)*, I got to brooding about the meaning of life and started reading the stuff on the Cheer box. Amazing. It contains ingredients to lift dirt from clothes (anionic surfactants) and soften water (complex sodium phosphates). Also, agents to protect washer parts (sodium silicate) and improve processing (sodium sulfate), small quantities of stuff to reduce wrinkling and prevent fabric yellowing, plus whiteners, colorant, and perfume. No kidding. All this for less than a nickel an ounce. It's biodegradable and works best in cold water—ecologically sound. A miracle in a box.

Sitting there watching the laundry go around in the dryer, I thought about the round world and hygiene. We've made a lot of progress, you know. We used to think that disease was an act of God. Then we figured out it was a product of human ignorance, so we've been cleaning up our act—literally—ever since. We've been getting the excrement off our hands and clothes and bodies and food and houses.

If only the scientific experts could come up with something to get it out of our minds. One cup of fixit frizzle that will lift the dirt from our lives, soften our hardness, protect our inner parts, improve our processing, reduce our yellowing and wrinkling, improve our natural color, and make us sweet and good.

Don't try Cheer, by the way. I tasted it. It's awful. *(But my tongue is clean now.)*

In reconsidering the Kindergarten book I was tempted to leave this story out. I don't do the laundry very much anymore. But sometimes I do—and for the same reason other people weed a garden or clean out a kitchen drawer. Doing a straightforward, clear-cut task that has a beginning and an end balances out the complexity-without-end that often vexes the rest of my life. Sacred simplicity.

And yes, I still stick things to my body with electricity. Poly-pro really works well. I once got everything in the dryer to cling to me long enough for me to walk through the kitchen and demonstrate my skill. It made my grandchildren laugh, which was the idea.

As to soap, I admit I've tried Bold, Power, Tide, True Grit, and Arm & Hammer—just because I like the notion of having muscle in my washing powder, and because I am a sucker for colorful packaging. Any old product that says "NEW AND IMPROVED" on it calls out to me.

I, too, hope to be New and Improved someday.

MEDICINE CABINETS

I WAS JUST WONDERING. Did you ever go to somebody's house for dinner or a party or something and then use the family bathroom? And while you were in there, did you ever take a look in the medicine cabinet? Just to kind of compare notes, you know? Didn't you ever—just look around—a little?

I have a friend who does it all the time. He claims he is doing research for a Ph.D. in sociology. He says lots of other people snoop in medicine cabinets, too. And they aren't working on a Ph.D. in sociology. It's not something people talk about much—because you think you might be the only one who is doing it, and you don't want people to think you're strange, right?

My friend says if you want to know the truth about people, the bathroom is the place to go. All you have to do is look in the drawers and shelves and cabinets. And take a look at the robes and pajamas and nightgowns hanging on the hook behind the door. You'll get the picture. He says all their habits and hopes and dreams and sorrows, illnesses and hang-ups, and even their sex life—all stand revealed in that one small room.

He says most people are secret slobs. He says the deepest

mysteries of the race are tucked into the nooks and crannies of the bathroom, where we go to be alone, to confront ourselves in the mirror, to comb and curry and scrape and preen our hides, to coax our aging and ailing bodies into one more day, to clean ourselves and relieve ourselves, to paint and deodorize our surfaces, to meditate and consult our oracle and attempt to improve our lot.

He says it's all there. In cans and bottles and tubes and boxes and vials. Potions and oils and unguents and sprays and tools and lotions and perfumes and appliances and soaps and pastes and pills and creams and pads and powders and medicines and devices beyond description—some electric and some not. The wonders of the ages.

He says he finds most bathrooms are about the same, and it gives him a sense of the wondrous unity of the human race.

I don't intend to start an epidemic of spelunking in people's bathrooms. But I did just go in and take a look in my own. I get the picture. I don't know whether to laugh or cry. There I am.

Go take a look. In your own Temple of Reality.

And from now on, please go to the bathroom at home before you visit me.

My bathroom is closed to the public.

JUMPER CABLES AND THE GOOD SAMARITAN

"HEY, YOU GOT JUMPER CABLES, buddy?"

"Yeah, sure. I got jumper cables."

English teacher and his nice sweet wife, from Nampa, Idaho (as I found out later). In their funny little foreign car. Drove around Seattle with their lights on in the morning fog, and left the lights on when they went for coffee, and so forth and so on. Dead meat now. Need jumper cables. Need Good Samaritan. Need a friendly hand from someone who looks like he knows what to do with jumper cables. And the Good Fairy of Fate placed them in my hands.

Men are supposed to know about jumper cables. It's supposed to be in the genetic code, right? But some of us men are mental mutants, and if it's under the hood of a car, well it's voodoo, Jack, and that's the end of it.

Besides, this guy only asked me if I *had* jumper cables. He didn't ask me if I knew how to *use* them. I thought by the way he asked that he knew what he was doing. After all, he had an Idaho license plate and was wearing a baseball cap and cowboy boots. All *those* people know about jumper cables when they're born, don't they? Guess he thought a white-bearded old man wearing hiking boots and driving a twenty-year-old VW van was bound to use jumper cables often and with authority.

So I get out my cables, and we swaggered around being all macho and cool and talking automobile talk. We look under the hood of his rig, and there's no battery.

"Hell," I said, "there's your problem right there. Somebody stole your battery."

"Dang," he said.

"The battery is under the backseat, dear," said his nice sweet wife.

"Oh."

So we took all the luggage and travel-junk out of the backseat and hauled the seat out into the parking lot and, sure enough, there it was. A battery. Right there. Just asking for jumper cables to be laid on it. I began to get worried when the guy smirked at his wife and said under his breath that he took auto mechanics and sex education at the same time in high school and they had been confused in his mind ever since, when it came to where things were and what you did to get any action out of them. We laughed. His wife didn't laugh at all. She just pulled out a manual and started thumbing through it.

Anyway, the sum of our knowledge was that positive poles and negative poles were involved, and either one or both cars ought to be running, and six-volt and twelve-volt batteries and other-volt batteries did or did not work out. I thought he knew what he was doing, and kind of went along with it. Guess he did the same. And we hooked it all up real tight and turned the ignition key in both cars at the same time. And there was this electrical arc between the cars that not only fried his ignition system, it welded the jumper cables to my battery and knocked the baseball cap off his head. The sound was like that of the world's largest fly hitting one of those electric killer screens. *ZISH*. Accompanied by an *awesome* blue flash and some smoke. Power is an amazing thing.

We just sat down right there in the backseat of his car, which was still sitting out in the parking lot. Awed by what we had accomplished. And his wife went off with the manual to find some semi-intelligent help. We talked as coolly and wisely as we could in the face of circumstances. He said, "Ignorance and power and pride are a deadly mixture, you know." English teachers talk like that.

"Sure are," I said. "Like matches in the hands of a three-year-old. Or automobiles in the hands of a sixteen-year-old. Or faith in God in the mind of a saint or a maniac. Or a nuclear arsenal in the hands of a movie character. Or even jumper cables and batteries in the hands of fools." *(We were trying to get something cosmic and serious out of our own invocation of power, you see. Humbled as we were.)*

Some time later I got a present in the mail from Nampa, Idaho. From the guy's nice sweet wife. As a gesture of grace— forgiveness combined with instruction and admonition to go and sin no more. What she sent was a set of electronic, true-start, foolproof, tangle-free jumper cables. Complete with instructions that tell you everything and more than you ever wanted to know about jumper cables in English and Spanish. The set is designed so that when you get everything all hooked up, a little solid-state switch control box tells you if you've done it right or not, before any juice flows. Gives you time to *think* if you really want to go ahead.

We could all use a device like that between us and power, I guess. It's nice to know that progress in such things is possible—in the face of ignorance and pride. Progress is possible. Next time he'll ask his wife first. Good Samaritans may be handy and enthusiastic, but if they are dumb, they aren't much help.

BAD SAMARITAN

Are you interested in humility avoidance and escaping a dumb death?

I can help.

Every time I do the same dimwit thing again, I mutter, *"I'll never learn."* As if acknowledging ignorance takes care of the problem. Yet, sometimes I get it straight—learn something by heart so firmly I'll take the knowledge with me to my grave. My most recent triumph:

If you woke me up out of a sound sleep in the middle of the night and shouted, "Battery Cables!" I'd sit up in bed and rap out my mantra:

"Separate and off. Red to good red. Red to bad red.
Black to good black. Black to engine block.
Start good car. Start bad car. Wait and reverse."

Be impressed. I've got this thing down. Nailed. Internalized. Never again will you find me standing by at a dead battery scene red-faced and ashamed of both my stupidity and what I'm about to go ahead and do anyhow.

The motivation? Humiliation. Again and again AND AGAIN, humiliation. Frying an ignition system or two. Getting zapped flat by jumping juice. Being laughed at by my grandchildren when I tried to help a stranded motorist. Finally, when I didn't stop to help a lady holding a scrawled sign saying "Dead battery—need help," and my wife gave me her what's-wrong-with-you lecture. Enough. It was time to stop being the Bad Samaritan.

I consulted several experts: a clerk at an auto parts emporium, a woman at a battery store, a driver for a AAA rescue truck, my friend Fred at my local gas station, and a seventeen year old kid who builds hotrods. They all gave me the same instructions. So, this is high-end information. Attend carefully—I will elaborate:

First, always use battery cables. Speaker wire or metal clothesline won't do.

Second, make sure the two cars are close, but not touching, with power off.

Third, attach red clamp to the good car battery on side of battery with +.

Fourth, attach red clamp to + side of bad battery.

Fifth, attach black clamp to − side of good battery.

Sixth, attach black clamp to engine block of car with dead battery.

(Why not to the minus side of the bad battery, you ask? If there is a spark when attaching the last cable, and the old battery is emitting fumes, you might cause an explosion and damage parts of you. Grounding the cable away from the battery avoids this possibility.)

When everything is connected, pray. Start the engine of the car with the good battery, wait a little, then start the car with the dead battery. Wait a little again to give the dead battery some life.

At this point, you may want to jump up and down, shout for joy, and thank Almighty God that it worked and nobody is dead or humiliated, most of all you. Then reverse the order in which you made the connections: black block off, black minus off, red bad off. Red good off.

If this doesn't work, call your mom. She probably knows more about what to do next than your dad does. He'll just give you a lot of voodoo moves that used to work on his old truck back when he was in high school. She'll tell you to call AAA or a tow truck.

Using modern memory techniques, I have reduced my mantra to even simpler information: "Aretha Franklin, the American Red Cross, and Death."

I can reconstruct the battery procedure from these three concepts. Consider: Aretha is famous for a tune called R-E-S-P-E-C-T, and that's the required mental attitude for this job—respect—electricity is dangerous. The American Red Cross, of course, is the place to begin—with the red cable at the positive plus sign. And death is what will happen if I don't remember to put the last black cable on a grounded place.

With my luck, though, I'll still panic. I can see me now, standing there in the rain on some dark and stormy night, trying to explain to some poor soul about how the battery cable deal depends on remembering "Lena Horne, the Salvation Army, and Severe Illness." "*What?*"

The Bad Samaritan strikes again.

BAR STORY

REAL EDUCATION comes in unexpected places. Real teachers know that.

When I began graduate school I needed a job—a night job— one that paid good money for short hours. Not easy to find. In desperation I accepted employment as a bartender in a hotel. Sounds OK, doesn't it? Any problem with being a bartender? Well, actually, yes. Or so I thought at the time.

Graduate school, in my case, was a theological seminary—a school for ministers. Working as a bartender could get me suspended from school. That's what I thought after I took the job. That's what my wife thought after I took the job. And my friends thought the same thing. Bad move.

In a defiant frame of mind I decided to turn myself in to the authorities at the school. Before the gossip got around I would just march into the dean's office and put it on the line: "I've got a job as a bartender. What are you going to do about it?"

The dean gave me his shrewdest look. A look I would learn over time to respect as an early warning sign of an educational experience.

"Wonderful," he exclaimed. "This is wonderful news."

"What?"

He explained that he and the faculty thought of me as young, green, arrogant, wet-behind-the-ears, inexperienced, and generally naïve about the real world. "Worse, you think you know everything."

Well, I *was* twenty-one.

He went on to explain that what was wrong with me could be fixed. What I needed to know most to become a minister was not something the school could teach me in a classroom. It wasn't in books. It wasn't in a church. What I needed to know was out there in the world.

As a bartender I would see many kinds of people with many kinds of needs. It would be a challenge to be useful and do my job and keep my values at the same time. Finally, the dean explained that being a minister was to be where you were really needed—not just safely yammering away in a pulpit on Sunday morning. Most bars could use a minister, he thought.

"Jesus," he said, "did not spend much time in church. He was out in the world."

The dean had a plan. He would consider my bartending job as a work-study program. A course in Life 101. Every Monday I would come in for an hour's conversation with him. He would ask what I had learned behind the bar. As long as I was learning something meaningful, I could get course credit.

"Keep your eyes open. Suspend judgment. Be useful," were his final instructions.

I tended bar for almost three years. The learning never ended. I discovered how willing people were to tell their life stories to a bartender. Not only did they have great problems, they sometimes had great solutions.

Not many ministers have Bartending 101, 102, and 103 as part of their education. When I graduated three years later, the dean gave me a fine evaluation. I had passed the bartending test. I knew a lot more about the world.

He did make one troubling comment: "Fulghum is not as good as he thinks he is."

"*What?*"

"Don't worry," he said, "be patient. In time you may be *better* than you think you are. Keep your eyes open. Suspend judgment. Be useful."

HELP

SAME MAN. Dean Bartlett. This time it's a couple of months before graduation. The pressure of studies had forced me to give
up my bartending job, and there were no immediate prospects for
a job after seminary. I had a wife and a baby son. I was flat broke
for the first time in my life. I was scared.

I went to the dean to explain my plight and ask for help.

Once again he surprised me.

"Wonderful," he exclaimed. "This is wonderful news."

"What?"

"You are a stubbornly proud young man. You are indepen-
dent to a fault. Nothing really wrong with that in itself, but we
thought you would never learn how or when to ask anyone for
help. How can you be a minister—be in the profession of helping
others—if you don't know what it's like to need help yourself?
Now you know how it feels to have to ask."

He paused to let that powerful admonition sink in.

"We will help you. You are worth helping. And before I go on,
think about how you felt when I said that. Lovely words. *We will
help you. You are worth helping.*"

Lesson Two for the day.

Dean Bartlett explained the next step for me was to prepare and submit a budget. Give the budget to his secretary, come back the next day, and help would be ready in the form of a check.

Greatly relieved, I went home and carefully crafted a tight-but-reasonable budget. Took the budget to the secretary. Went back the next day for the check.

"Sorry," she said, "but the dean says your budget is unacceptable."

I felt bad about that. I must have asked for too much. So I revised the budget downward to a bread-and-water and rent-and-utilities level. Took the budget back to the secretary. Returned the next day. No check.

"Sorry," she said, "but the dean says your budget is still unacceptable."

Angry and confused, I opened the dean's office door without knocking, and unloaded my frustration on him. "You said you'd help me. You said I was worth helping. But you won't accept my budget. You know I can't live on less. What the hell is going on?"

He smiled. "Wonderful," he said. "Just wonderful."

I collapsed in a chair, realizing I was going to learn something again.

"Now that your fit is over, would you like to know exactly *why* your budget is unacceptable to me and this educational institution?"

"Yes."

"Listen to me carefully: *There is nothing in your budget for joy*. No books, no flowers, no music, not even a cold beer. And there is nothing in your budget to give away to someone else. *We don't help people who don't have better values than you do.*"

WHAM!

Nothing for joy.

Nothing to give away.

No help for people who don't have better values than I.

Lesson Three. Lesson learned.

There was much joy in my next budget. The dean approved it. But it wasn't until I told someone else this story that I realized that what I had to give away was this story itself.

STUFF

MOVING IS A BLOW to my self-image. I like to think I am reasonably clean and tidy. But comes that moment after all the furniture and possessions have been removed from my rooms, and I come back to see if I've left anything, and I look at the floor and there's all this STUFF around. Behind where the desk was, and behind where the bookcase was, and behind where the bed was, and in the corner once occupied by the chest-of-drawers.

Stuff. Gray. Fuzzy. Hairy. Grotty. Stuff.

Look at all that dirt, I think. I am not so very nice and clean after all, I think. What would the neighbors think? I think. What would my mother say? I think. What if *they* come to inspect? I think. I got to clean it up quick, I think. This Stuff. It's *always* there when I move. *What is it?*

I read in a medical journal that a laboratory analyzed this Stuff. They were working on the problems of people with allergies, but their results apply here.

The findings: particles of wool, cotton, and paper, bug chunks, food, plants, tree leaves, ash, microscopic spores of fungi and single-celled animals, and a lot of unidentifiable odds and ends, mostly natural and organic.

But that's just the miscellaneous list. The majority of Stuff comes from just two sources: *people*—exfoliated skin and hair; and *meteorites*—disintegrated as they hit the earth's atmosphere. *(No kidding—it's true—tons of it fall every day.)* In other words, what's behind my bed and bookcase and dresser and chest is mostly me and stardust.

A botanist told me that if you gather up a bunch of Stuff in a jar and put some water in it and let it sit in the sunlight and then plant a seed in it, the seed will grow like crazy; or if you do the same thing but put it in a damp, dark place, mushrooms will grow in it. And then, if you eat the mushrooms, you may see stars.

Also, if you really want to see a lot of it, take the sheet off your bed, shake it hard in a dark room, and then turn on a beamed flashlight. There you are. Like the little snowman in the round glass ball on the mantel at Grandma's house. London Bridge is falling down and I am falling down and the stars are falling down. And everything else is falling down, to go around again, some say.

Scientists have pretty well established that we come from a stellar birthing room.

We are the Stuff of stars.

And there behind my desk, I seem to be returning to my source, in a quiet way. Recombining with the Stuff of the universe into who-knows-what. And I've a heightened respect for what's going on in the nooks and crannies of my room.

It isn't dirt. It's all compost. Cosmic compost.

VACUUMS

A MAN I HAD NOT SEEN in years stopped me on the street recently. He once was a nodding-acquaintance neighbor who lived up at the end of the block. "How's business?" I asked, and he came back with "Business really sucks!" and laughed. I knew he was going to say this. It's been his trademark quip for years. He's a regional sales manager for a vacuum cleaner company. His humor is tacky, but I like his enthusiasm and the confidence he has in his product line.

"Anything you want to suck up or blow away, anywhere, anytime, we got the machine," he says. HandiVac, ShopVac, SuperVac and specialty rigs to clean out chimneys and furnaces. He's got built-in systems for whole buildings, vacuum cleaners to slurp up chemical and oil pollutants. And he's got blowers—leaf blowers, grass blowers, and underwater trash blower systems for pools. Indoors, outdoors, on the ground, in the sea, or in the sky—no task too big or small. It's a large company and he's been their gold-medal salesman for years.

"Stand back, give me AIR!" is his war cry.

His personal hero is a man named James Murry Spengler. In

1907 Spengler was a janitor in a department store in Ohio. But he was going to have to give up his job because the mechanical carpet sweeper he had to use kicked up so much dust and mold, he had developed chronic allergy problems. So Spengler solved his problem by inventing the first vacuum cleaner.

You'd laugh to see the original model—made out of a pillowcase, a soapbox, a fan, and yards of tape. Still, the device not only worked, it solved Spengler's allergy problems and saved his career as a janitor. You've never heard of Spengler because he sold the patent to a man whose name you do know, William Hoover.

My friend the salesman reveres Spengler because he took common items he found at home and, using the most obvious natural resource, *air*, he changed domestic history. I don't know how many times I've heard this story from my former neighbor. When he told it to me one more time last week, I couldn't resist asking him if he was still a hypocrite.

He blushed. Smiled. "Yes."

Perhaps hypocrite is not quite the right word. Maybe "philosopher."

I'll explain the accusation and you can decide.

Early on in our neighbor experience, I noticed a profound contradiction in the life of this air salesman. It puzzled me. I'd be out in my yard and would look up and see him mowing his yard with an old hand-powered push mower. Then he would pile up the grass clippings using an equally old-fashioned hand rake. Finally, he would sweep his sidewalk and driveway with a classic straight broom and pick up the piles with a dustpan. In the fall he raked his leaves by hand—no blower. And when he tidied his car, he swept it out with a whisk-broom. Where was all the machinery that sucked things up and blew things away?

One day I confronted him and he confessed.

ROBERT FULGHUM

He had once tried to sell his wares to an Amish farmer in Iowa whose religious and social values did not allow the use of electricity and gasoline engines. The Amish believe that those things that do not serve the family, the community, or the individual well should be avoided. Noisy engines separate people and make it hard for them to sing together while they work, and even harder to think when they work alone. Hand tools are cheap, easy to repair, and give the user good exercise. Speed and efficiency do not always increase the quality of life.

When my friend's life gets to be too much of an air raid and he needs sanity, he remembers the Amish. He goes out into his yard with his hand tools for an afternoon of seeking wisdom in simplicity. A noisy machine won't help when his soul feels empty. In his middle years he has acquired the wisdom of choosing appropriate technology. Pushing leaves with mechanical air is not the same as hearing the wind blow through the trees.

THE MERMAID

GIANTS, WIZARDS, AND DWARFS was the game to play. Being left in charge of about eighty children seven to ten years old, while their parents were off doing parenty things, I mustered my troops in the church social hall and explained the game. It's a large-scale version of Rock, Paper, and Scissors, and involves some intellectual decision-making. But the real purpose of the game is to make a lot of noise and run around chasing people until nobody knows which side you are on or who won.

Organizing a roomful of wired-up grade-schoolers into two teams, explaining the rudiments of the game, achieving consensus on group identity—all this is no mean accomplishment, but we did it with a right good will and were ready to go.

The excitement of the chase had reached a critical mass. I yelled out: "You have to decide *now* which you are—a GIANT, a WIZARD, or a DWARF!"

While the groups huddled in frenzied, whispered consultation, a tug came at my pants leg. A small child stands there looking up, and asks in a small, concerned voice, "Where do the Mermaids stand?"

Where do the Mermaids stand?

A long pause. A *very* long pause. "Where do the Mermaids stand?" says I.

"Yes. You see, I am a Mermaid."

"There are no such things as Mermaids."

"Oh, yes, I am one!"

She did not relate to being a Giant, a Wizard, or a Dwarf. She knew her category. Mermaid. And was not about to leave the game and go over and stand against the wall where a loser would stand. She intended to participate, wherever Mermaids fit into the scheme of things. Without giving up dignity or identity. She took it for granted that there was a place for Mermaids and that I would know just where.

Well, where *do* the Mermaids stand? All the "Mermaids"—all those who are different, who do not fit the norm and who do not accept the available boxes and pigeonholes?

Answer that question and you can build a school, a nation, or a world on it.

What was my answer at the moment? Every once in a while I say the right thing. "The Mermaid stands right here by the King of the Sea!" says I.

So we stood there hand in hand, reviewing the troops of Wizards and Giants and Dwarfs as they roiled by in wild disarray.

It is not true, by the way, that mermaids do not exist.

I know at least one personally.

I have held her hand.

TAXI

NEW YORK CITY. Winter. Corner of 52nd Street and Madison Avenue. Cold and wildly windy. Traffic jammed-slammed tight. An ill-tempered mood plagues the streets. But me, I'm waving politely at taxis. Clearly, I'm from out of town.

Yellow Cab eases up in front of me. The driver, a massive Black lady wearing a pink nylon jacket and black turban, barks at me—a don't-mess-with-me-expression on her face: "You want a ride or a date or what?" Yes, I want a ride, so I get in the back seat. She turns and barks at me again. "So. Just where're you going, my man?"

"I'm going uptown. Ninety-First and Fifth."

She laughs. "Not with me, you ain't."

"Why not?"

"The city is set like cement. Must be a fifty-foot brick wall across midtown. This town's always locked up for something. A parade of anything—retired dogcatchers, the Ku Klux Klan, dentists, who knows what? Could be His Blessitude the Pope is still here. Could be the president is back in town. Could be Jesus Christ hisself, for all I know. He's about the only one who hasn't been here this year."

She laughs again. Big laugh.

"So, I can't get uptown?"

"Not in this cab—not unless you go around by way of Chicago. But I'll take you downtown as far as you want to go—Wall Street, New Jersey, Florida, or Rio de Janeiro. I mean as *far* as you want to go, my man. We could have some fun going downtown. But not *uptown*. No way today."

"Thanks. I like your turban, by the way. What country are you from?"

Big laugh. "The turban is just my hat. I'm from the country of New York City. Bred here, born here, grew up here, still live here, can't get away from here, and going to die here. But I keep thinking—somehow, someday—I'm leaving. But I know I'm dreaming. Maybe they'll stuff me and put me in a museum with a sign under me that says here's the dumbest broad who ever lived—she should have left New York a long time ago and was too slow to go."

"How come you don't leave?"

"Ain't you got a list of things you shoulda done a long time ago?"

"Yes."

"Well, there's your *why*, my man, and all the *why* there is. Who knows? Besides, it's dangerous and weird outside New York. Tornadoes and the woods on fire and bears and rednecks and born-agains and slow-talking people and beauty queens and cowboys and Indians and all that. I'd rather take my chances in New York."

"You still don't look very happy about it."

"Well, I've had a bad day, my man. Like I say, town's locked up—like somebody spilled glue on a cockroach convention. Weather's bad but not bad enough—too many people walking. The cab is running rough and my boyfriend has run off with two other women—not one, but *two*. And my rent's way overdue. God is definitely not on my side. But, hey, rain's over—you gonna talk or ride?"

"I should pay you just to drive me around and talk to me. But I've go to go uptown to a meeting, so I'll get out." Standing by her door, I make an offer: "Here's twenty dollars—a gift—to balance out a bad day."

"Twenty dollars? It's not enough."

"Not enough?"

"If you think twenty dollars will pull me even with the craziness of New York City and the wrath of Almighty God, then you're weirder than you look and you need the money more than I do. Here, take it."

"How much would pull you even?"

She thinks in amused silence, laughs, holds out her hand.

"There's not enough money in the universe. Here, gimme that twenty. If I don't take what I *can* get, I'll never get *nothing*. I'm grateful, my man." Honking and waving and laughing, she charged off into the impossible traffic more like the driver of a tank than a taxi—just possibly working her way uptown or beyond. Somehow. Someday. Onward.

Attitude. It's all attitude.

Another mermaid.

SUMMER JOB

Two desperate young men were at my door one night last week. "We're desperate," they said. They didn't look desperate. Neat and clean—tennis shoes, jeans, T-shirts, and baseball caps on the right way. "We're fifteen years old," which is why they were desperate. They needed summer jobs and nobody was hiring unless you were sixteen. "Being fifteen isn't good enough," said one. I remember. Being fifteen is being in-between—a transitional phase.

"Just how desperate are you?" I asked.

"Really desperate—we'll do anything for money."

Wonderful. Actually I had been looking for a couple of guys in this condition. See, a neighbor has been needling me about my excessive firewood. He thinks it weighs too much and is maybe bending the timbers of the decking on the dock in front of our houseboats, and since the dock decking is common property, it's his business. Furthermore, he thinks that burning wood in a stove contributes to serious air pollution problems and I am therefore irresponsible for not heating my house some other way. Right. I agree. That's exactly why I have so much firewood: I don't burn it anymore. But this guy keeps yawping at me and I'm steamed.

Suddenly I have a genius solution for the firewood fracas.

"Gentlemen," I say to the young men at my door, "I have a job for you." They are excited. "You see all this firewood along the dock?"

"Yes."

"Well, I want you to haul it all up onto the street where you will find my neighbor's very large four-door green Buick sedan. And I want you to fill that Buick with this firewood."

"There's too much to go in the trunk, sir."

"Exactly. So, I want you to fill the whole inside of the Buick completely with firewood—door to door and floor to ceiling. And if you have any left over I want you to stack it on the hood and roof. Doing it carefully, of course."

"We couldn't do that sir—we might get in trouble."

"How about if I pay you ten dollars each and you do it at night?"

"We could do that, sir. But what if we get caught?"

"For an extra five dollars apiece you will not get caught."

"Right, sir."

"And besides," I tell them, "at fifteen you're still juveniles—they won't give you the electric chair for misplacing a pile of firewood. Do it."

I am tired of being patient and reasonable and fussing around with the minutiae of life. Direct-and-swift action is my mode these days. A one-man SWAT team am I. Don't mess with me. My neighbor is lucky I didn't pile up the wood on his front porch and set it on fire. After all, who would believe that a nice man like me would do such a thing? I've worked hard all these years on my disguise of benign gentleness and the time has come for the Bad Samaritan to rip off his mask and strike.

So the neighbor is away for the weekend. And I happen to know where he keeps his hide-a-key: in a really dumb place under the rear bumper of his Buick—I saw him put it there. I make sure his car is unlocked, and during the night I hear the lovely sound of firewood being moved by desperate fifteen year-olds.

The next morning I am pleased to find the wood gone. And the Buick looks like a movable wood yard. Ha. Brilliant. I'm thinking my neighbor is going to have a cow when he gets home. Funny.

Did this really happen?

Yes and No. The young men did come to the door. The neighbor and the firewood are real. And the whole scenario did flash through my mind. The thing even went as far as the midnight moment. And there was a time in my life when I would have gone through with it.

But now. Well. I am, alas, older and wiser. Too bad.

I stopped the young men. Paid them. But I had considered that my neighbor is a cunning devil with a wicked sense of humor. He would have got even. He would have paid the young men to stack the firewood in my bathroom. Not so funny.

Maybe I'm going through a desperate transitional phase like I did at age fifteen. I often have these loony ideas and come close to acting on them.

But. Maybe. And However.

The imagined memory must suffice sometimes.

If you only make it up, you never have to live it down.

WEISER, IDAHO

I ONCE SPENT a week in Weiser, Idaho.

Maybe that's hard to believe. Because if you've ever looked at an Idaho map, you know Weiser is nowhere. But if you play the fiddle, Weiser, Idaho, is the center of the universe. The Grand National Old Time Fiddlers' Contest is there the last week in June. And since I've fiddled around some in my time, I went.

Four thousand people live there in normal times. Five thousand more come out of the bushes and trees and hills for the contest. The town stays open around the clock, with fiddling in the streets, dancing at the VFW hall, fried chicken in the Elks Lodge, and free camping at the rodeo grounds.

People from all over show up—fiddlers from Pottsboro, Texas; Sepulpa, Oklahoma; Thief River Falls, Minnesota; Caldwell, Kansas; Three Forks, Montana; and just about every other little crossroads town you care to mention. And even Japan and Ireland and Nova Scotia!

It used to be that the festival was populated by country folks—pretty straight types—short hair, church on Sunday, overalls and gingham, and all that. Then the long-haired hippie freaks began to show up. The trouble was that the freaks could fiddle to beat hell. And that's all there was to it.

So, the town turned over the junior high school and its grounds to the freaks. The contest judges were put in an isolated room where they could only hear the music. Couldn't see what people looked like or what their names were—just hear the fiddling. As one old gentleman put it, "Son, I don't care if you're stark nekkid and wear a bone in your nose. If you kin fiddle, you're all right with me. It's the music we make that counts."

So I was standing there in the middle of the night in the moonlight in Weiser, Idaho, with about a thousand other people who were picking and singing and fiddling together—some with bald heads, some with hair to their knees, some with a joint, some with a long-necked bottle of Budweiser, some with beads, some with Archie Bunker T-shirts, some eighteen and some eighty, some with corsets and some with no bras, and the music rising like incense into the night toward whatever gods of peace and goodwill there may be. I was standing there, and this policeman—a real honest-to-god on-duty Weiser policeman—who is standing next to me and *picking a banjo (really, I swear it)*—says to me, "Sometimes the world seems like a fine place, don't it?"

Yes.

Don't believe me? Go see for yourself. Weiser's still there. The festival still happens. They still don't care what you look like. It's the music that counts.

BIBLE STORY

A s a former high school teacher, I'm often invited to reunions. Sometimes the reunions are very private—one-on-one—as happened last week. While a student was in town for a class gathering he called to ask: "Could we get together for a cup of coffee? I have something to get off my chest."

His confession cleared up a long-standing mystery. In his senior year he had called me at home on a Sunday afternoon to say that he knew I was a parish minister and he had an urgent religious question to ask. Serious possibilities passed through my mind—"Sure, go ahead."

"Mr. Fulghum, do you know how to clean puke out of a Bible?"

"What?"

"It's awful—I just can't tell you—but I've got to do something before my mother gets home tonight." I couldn't help him. There are some things not covered in seminary. I admit to being chicken-hearted. A prudent man avoids a mess like this.

On Monday I asked what was going on, but he said that I wouldn't really want to know. Now, ten years later, comes the truth. His parents were away for the weekend. And he had done *exactly* what they told him *not to do*: had some friends over for a party. Of course. There was beer. A girl drank too much, lay down on the bed in his mom's room, and tossed her cookies. Trying not to throw up in the bed, she aimed over the side and hosed the nightstand. On the nightstand lay the mother's Bible. Open.

All evidence of the party could be cleaned up. Except the mess on the Bible.

Desperate, our tragic young hero wrapped the evidence in a plastic bag.

He buried it in the back yard.

He bought his Mom a new Bible, and told some terrible lie about borrowing hers for a school project and losing it on a bus. She was really mad, but not nearly as mad as she might have been if she knew the truth. He could handle his mom's wrath. She would never know. But he knew God knew, and he was sure God was going to get him. The experience kept him out of trouble and in church for the rest of his senior year.

Now, ten years later he still hasn't told his mother the truth. He still thinks she would kill him if she knew. It wasn't just any old Bible. It was the Family Bible—passed down from his grandmother to his mother. And the Bible is still out there in the yard somewhere. Of course, he's forgotten *exactly* where by now, but if he knew he would sneak home sometime when his mother was away and dig it up. But, of course, he wouldn't be able to explain why the backyard was full of small craters.

"Well," I said, after laughing myself limp, "the only thing I can do for you is to give you an example of the things adults and teachers and parents do that are just about as awful. At least you will know you have company." I told him my tale.

That same spring I had a very full teaching load. My classroom was on the third floor and the nearest men's toilet was three floors down. In desperate circumstances one morning in the middle of a class, I excused myself, walked swiftly down the hall into a closet to use the janitor's sink. But the sink had a sign on it, saying "Does Not Drain." Panicked and about to explode I used a large plastic bucket that was handy. Snapping the lid on the bucket I moved it into an art supplies storage closet—I had the only key.

Alas, the convenience of this solution to my problem was too easy not to use again another day. By the end of the week, however, I had a different problem: what to do with a bucket containing a rather amazing amount of urine?

Late one afternoon, long after school was out, I tried sneaking down the stairs with the bucket to empty it in the toilet three floors down. I stumbled on the stairs. And let go of the bucket. Which sailed through the air and exploded like a mortar shell into the hallway. True.

Disgusting. Yes. Stupid. Yes. Go ahead, beat me up over this— a nice man like me. Tell me you never did anything dumb or gross in your entire life. Tell me you never had to clean up your own mess. Besides, what I did was not illegal, immoral, or a sin. Just *stupid*. The Bible says those without guilt should throw the first stone.

It took a couple of hours to mop up the mess. And a couple of bottles of air cleaner to kill the smell. When people complained the next day that something awful seemed to have happened in the hall overnight, I kept my mouth shut. And have, until now.

"Welcome back to the best part of the reunion," I said to the Bible-burier—"where the truth can finally be told." Maybe, someday, his mother will tell him things she did behind his back. Then they can they dig up the backyard looking for her Bible.

THE NAMES OF THINGS

Anybody seen a Naked Broomrape, a Bastard Toad-flax, a Lesser Dirty Socks, or a Crouching Locoweed? These items are listed in various field guides to the wildflowers of North America. I am not making up these names. I can show you the photographs, too. Trying to mitigate my ignorance and to stop asking "What's that?" of anybody I go hiking with, I've been working my way through the field guides and stumbling over these wiggy labels. My suspicions are aroused. Do these flowers with the bizarre names really exist, or is there some conspiracy among botanists to pull the public's leg?

If the plants are really out there, then I'd give a prize to meet the yahoos responsible for sticking such miserable names on nature's blooming flora. How could you look at a flowering plant and say, "Let's call that sucker a Naked Broomrape"? Especially when the purported flower has a pale violet trumpet shape with a dab of purest yellow in the center. You've got to be in a bad mood to do that.

Worse, I want to get a look at the crab who had the peevish gall to say, "Well, that looks like a Bastard Toad-flax to me." The actual plant is small, the complex flowers pale ivory, and the leaves olive green. Come on.

And someone must have had a bad day in the bush when they declared, "See that—I say that sorry sonofabitch deserves to be called a Crouching Locoweed." Referring to a plant with slender leaves, bearing a tall flower with multiple silvery-white petals.

And as for "Dirty Socks"—a pinkish flower with touches of purple in the middle—I'd like to see the socks of the one who did the christening. I've seen ugly and unlaundered socks on some hikers, but I wouldn't stick the name on a plant.

All I can figure is that some plant mavens have a sour sense of respect for the subjects of their vocation. Field guides are full of mean-spirited adjectives—the "lowly" this, the "false" that, the "dwarf" whatnot and the "pygmy" something else. Wonder what they name their dogs and cats and children?

And I'd sure like to know what was going on in the mind of the guy who named a small yellow sunflower the "Nipple Seed." I'd like to meet his girlfriend, too. If he ever had one.

So who cares, really? There are lots better things to get stirred up about, aren't there? I suppose political correctness in naming wildflowers is not a bandwagon with much steam behind it, though dumber matters do get a lot of press.

But I do wonder what would happen if we were to wipe the slate clean of all the names for things around us and start over. If our generation were responsible for labeling the environment, would we do any better, be any kinder to our plant friends? Probably not. Can you imagine the meetings—the congressional hearings?

Besides, the experts tell us that the evolution of living things continues at such a rate that plants and animals and insects come into and go out of existence faster than human beings can catalog them. The number of living things we have identified and named is far outnumbered by those we don't even know about. Most of what we have named is dead and gone, actually. There may have been a Naked Broomrape once, but it may be extinct by now. Something else will take its place. And we get to name that one. Better job next time.

And sometimes we actually do a better job. My favorites from the field guides are the Rosy Pussytoes, the Enchanter's Nightshade, and the Chocolate Lily. Progress.

I wonder what flowers would call us? Creeping Fat Farm Fungus? Deadly Sucker Bush? Night-Screaming Doodlebugs? Weeping Wooky Weeds?

Almost every living species has been here far longer than ours—the fossil evidence is clear. And many will likely be here long after we've wandered off into the doomsday dustbin ourselves, still sticking names on things as we went. Scientists tell us the Earth has been around 4.5 billion years and has another 5.7 billion to go.

What does a flower care about what label we apply in passing? The labels only stick to us.

WATER

"**W**HAT KIND OF WATER WILL YOU HAVE?" A question asked by my hostess at a dinner party. She offered fizzy or flat, French or Italian, mountain glacial or deep artesian. I could also choose natural or flavored, iced or room temperature, with lime wedge or lemon twist.

Actually, I was surprised at the somewhat limited choices offered by my hostess. Our corner grocery store alone carries thirty-one brands of bottled water—from sources in France, Canada, Wales, Germany, Italy, and Norway, as well as the USA. Even the island of Fiji. The water comes from ancient springs, high mountain streams, and mineralized deposits. Three colors of bottles—clear, sea green, and deep blue—and all with elegant labeling.

This so-called "designer water" has taken its fair share of abuse for appearing to be a pretentious extravagance. But the same criticism could be made of the marketing of beer, wine, and hard liquor. Or even films and novels and music. The appeal is to the imagination—to the romantic side of human nature.

I like fancy water.

90

I'm delighted to drink a glass of liquid that began as snow in the French Alps hundreds of years before I was born, then became ice in a glacier, melted into deep underground springs, and finally was bottled and hauled all the way across sea and land to sit available on my grocer's shelf.

For a very small price, I can have a reflective reverie in a glass—an ordinary glass that reveals the wonders of nature, the inventiveness of the industrial revolution and the pleasures of a poetic view of life.

Moreover, this liquid is good for me. It is me, as a matter of fact—90 percent of my body is water. I'm please to have my essential juices get an occasional transfusion of fanciful pizzazz.

There is a high end of the water market as yet untouched: rare and historic water. I'm thinking beyond natural purity—of water that has value because of its age or its association with special events or because there simply is no more of it ever to be had. This is the fine-wine division of bottled water.

A few examples: Several years ago, a former student brought me a liter of water all the way from the spring at Delphi in Greece—a source from which the noble Greeks of the fourth century drank when they went to consult the oracles of fate. I drink a little on April Fool's Day.

One Christmas my wife gave me a bottle of water from the creek we hike alongside in summer. She had carefully filtered the water and filled the bottle on my birthday. I've great memories of fine days in that valley. We drank a toast with the water during our Christmas dinner—a toast to past happiness and present joy.

I know a man who saved a bottle of Colorado River water from the days when the river ran free—before the Glen Canyon Dam turned it into a silty lake. That bottle sits on a shelf in his office in a place of honor—marking both his younger days and the time of an American West that's gone forever. Sometimes he smiles when he sees it. Sometimes it brings tears to his eyes.

Once I participated in a christening ceremony that used baptismal water that had been collected from the rain dripping off the fly of a tent during the camping weekend when the couple conceived their first child.

And I attended a first anniversary dinner celebration of an April wedding that had been turned into a magical occasion by an unexpected snowfall. The bride's father had collected the melting snow and now brought the bottle of water as an anniversary gift. Priceless.

There's no commercial value in water of this kind. There are two secret ingredients, which can't be manufactured or bottled: imagination and memory. Such vintage refreshment is always a product of home brewing. The liquid is flavored by experience and given character by the creative effort it takes to fill the wine cellar of the heart.

Let the glasses be filled and lifted—Cheers!

THIRD AID

M Y WIFE HAS TRIED for some time to get me to read news stories about people who live long and healthy lives. She's a doctor. And a semi-vegetarian. She's excited about studies of isolated groups of people who dwell twelve thousand feet up in the Andes or way out in the Russian boondocks. They eat chickpeas and gravel, and walk six miles a day to get water. Shriveled up old prunish people whose life secret seems to be that they never change clothes or take baths. Not my idea of a long and happy life. They look ugly and unhappy and bored. I don't want to be one of them. Or married to anybody like them, either.

I think long life is as overrated as natural childbirth. I'll pass on both of them. Most of the really old people I've known are a royal pain in the butt. Oh, sure, tell me about your sainted mother or your wonderful great-grandfather and how they lived to be 150 years old. I said, "most."

My personal plan is called Third Aid.

Not First Aid. That's what you do in immediate crises. If you cut yourself, you spend a half hour looking all over the house for a Band-Aid and settle for Scotch tape.

Second Aid is calling the doctor because you've got the flu. By the time you actually get in for a checkup, the flu is gone. While you've been waiting, you've got some extra sleep, been patted on the head, taken some aspirin, and eaten some chicken soup. You're cured.

Third Aid is my version of preventive medicine—so you don't need as much First and Second Aid. I read through my wife's medical-school textbooks. And I noticed that in just about every crisis the drill was the same: have the patient lie down in a comfortable place, make sure the patient can breathe, make sure the patient isn't bleeding, and is kept warm and dry. I think this is called the ABC checkup—for Airway, Blood, and Comfort or something like that.

In addition to this ABC business, I read about the Placebo Effect. That's where no matter what you do, anywhere from 30 to 60 percent of what gets wrong with you heals itself if you just give it time and think good thoughts. It's kind of like staying amused while your body does its thing. See, doctors can really do something with only about 15 percent of what ails you. Your body does the rest. Or else you die.

If you want to practice Third Aid, what do you do?

First, realize *your body makes house calls—so does your brain*. This is crucial.

Every once in awhile, when you're not sick, lie down and examine yourself.

Ask yourself three questions: Am I breathing? Am I bleeding? And am I comfy? If your answers are Yes, No, and Yes, you're going to live a while longer. Then ask: Am I hungry? Am I thirsty? Is there anything in the house to eat?

If yes, eat and drink. If not, don't.

This is important: If you know something isn't necessary or isn't good for you, don't get up and do it. If you do it anyhow, don't complain about it, just lie down and shut up and wait. It's elemental: *When in doubt, get down*. Take a nap.

Try reading a human body manual—you'd do as much for your car, why not your body? I read that 90 percent of doctors' visits depend on their giving attention and getting our trust. I figure if I pay attention to myself and trust my body, I don't have to bother the doctor.

But, suppose I have something serious and really need a doctor?

I'm personally ambivalent about calling on a doctor. I live with one.

I'm told that most of us will die in a hospital bed hooked up to tubes and wires. Not me. I want my body to go before my brain. I want to die at a dance or a delicatessen—from too much fun or food.

Of course I won't live to be a hundred.

So, who would want me to?

YELLING

IN THE SOLOMON ISLANDS in the South Pacific some villagers practice a unique form of logging. If a tree is too large to be felled with an ax, the natives cut it down by yelling at it. *(Can't lay my hands on the article, but I swear I read it.)* Woodsmen with special powers creep up on a tree just at dawn and suddenly scream at it at the top of their lungs. They continue this for thirty days. The tree dies and falls over. The theory is that the hollering kills the spirit of the tree. According to the villagers, it always works.

Ah, those poor naïve innocents. Such quaintly charming habits of the jungle. Screaming at trees, indeed. How primitive. Too bad they don't have the advantages of modern technology and the scientific mind.

Me? I yell at my wife. And yell at the telephone and the lawn mower. And yell at the TV and the newspaper and my children. I've even been known to shake my fist and yell at the sky at times.

Man next door yells at his car a lot. And this summer I heard him yell at a stepladder for most of an afternoon. We modern, urban, educated folks yell at traffic and umpires and bills and banks and machines—especially machines. Machines and relatives get most of the yelling. But never trees.

Don't know what good it does. Machines and things just sit there. Even kicking doesn't always help. As for people, well, the Solomon Islanders may have a point. Yelling at living things does tend to kill the spirit in them.

Sticks and stones may break our bones, but words will break our hearts. . . .

DONNIE

THE RAP ON THE DOOR was sharp, urgent, insistent—a fore-boding of crisis—rappity-rappityrappity *rap* . . . Me, rushing to the door, fumbling with the lock, pumping my adrenaline, preparing for an emergency. What? What? What?

Small boy. Odd expression. Hands me a scrawled note on much-folded paper: "My name is Donnie. I will rake your leaves. $1 a yard. I am deaf. You can write to me. I can read. I rake good."

(Across the back of our house is a row of middle-aged ma-tronly maple trees, extravagantly dressed in season in a million leaf-sequins. And in season the sequins detach. Not much wind in our sheltered yard, so the leaves lie about the ladies' feet now like dressing gowns they've stepped out of in preparation for the bath of winter.

I like the way it looks. I like the way it looks very much. My wife does not. The gardening magazine does not like it, either. Leaves should be raked. There are rules. Leaves are not good for grass. Leaves are untidy. Leaves are moldyslimy. But I like leaves so much, I once filled my classroom at school ankle-deep with them.

There is a reason for leaves. There is no reason for mowed grass. So say I.

My wife does not see it this way. There is an unspoken accusation in the air of laziness. We have been through this before. But this year a bargain has been struck in the name of the Scientific Method. Half the yard will be properly raked, and the other half will be left in the care of nature. Come summer, we shall see. And so her part is raked and mine is not. Let it be.)

Like a pilot in a fog relying on limited instruments, the boy looks intently at my face for information. He knows I have leaves. He has seen them. Mine is the *only* yard in the neighborhood with leaves, in fact. He knows his price is right. Solemnly he holds out pencil and paper for my reply. How can I explain to him about the importance of the scientific experiment going on in my backyard?

(In a way, the trees are there because of the leaves. With unbridled extravagance, zillions of seeds have helicoptered out of the sky to land like assault forces to green the earth. The leaves follow to cover, protect, warm, and nourish the next generation of trees. Stony ground, rot, mold, bacteria, birds, squirrels, bugs, and people—all intervene. But somehow, some make it. Some tenacious seeds take hold and hold on and hold on—for dear life. In the silence of winter's dark they prevail and plant themselves and survive to become the next generation of trees. It has been thus for eons, and we mess with the process at our peril, say I. This is important.)

"My name is Donnie. I will rake your leaves. $1 a yard. I am deaf. You can write to me. I can read. I rake good." He holds out the pencil and paper with patience and hope and goodwill.

There are times when the simplest of events call all of one's existential motives into question. What would I do if he weren't deaf? What will it do for him if I say no? If I say yes? What difference? We stand in each other's long silence, inarticulate for different reasons. In the same motion, he turns to go and I reach for the pencil and paper to write, solemnly: "Yes. Yes, I would like to have my leaves raked." A grave nod from the attentive businessmanchild.

I write: "Do you do it when they are wet?"

"Yes," he writes.

"Do you have your own rake?"

"No."

"This is a big yard—there are lots of leaves."

"Yes."

"I think I should give you two dollars."

A smile. "Three?" he writes.

A grin.

Done. We have a contract. The rake is produced, and Donnie the deaf leaf-raker goes to work in the fast-falling November twilight. In silence he rakes. In silence I watch—through the window of the dark house. Are there any sounds at all in his mind? I wonder. Or only the hollow, empty sea-sound I get when I put my fingers in my ears as tightly as I can.

Carefully he rakes the leaves into a large pile, as instructed. *(Yes, I am thinking I will spread them out over the yard again after he is gone. I am stubborn about this.)* Carefully he goes back over the yard picking up missed leaves by hand and carrying them to the pile. He also is stubborn about *his* values. Raking leaves means *all* the leaves.

Signing that he must go because it is dark and he must go home to eat, he leaves the work unfinished. Having paid in advance, I wonder if he will return. At my age, I am cynical. Too cynical.

Come morning, he has returned to his task, first checking the previously raked yard for latecomers. He takes pride in his work. The yard is leaf-free. I note his picking up several of the brightest yellow leaves and putting them into the pocket of his sweat shirt. Along with a whole handful of helicoptered seeds.

Rappity-rappity-rappity-rap! He reports to the door, signing that the work is done. As he walks away up the street I see him tossing one helicoptered seed into the air at a time. Fringe benefits. I stand in my own door in my own silence, smiling at his grace. Fringe benefits.

Tomorrow I will go out and push the pile of leaves over the bank into the compost heap at the bottom of the ravine behind our house. I will do it in silence. The leaves and seeds will have to work out their destiny there this year. I could not feel right about undoing his work. My experiment with science will have to stand aside for something more human. The leaves let go, the seeds let go, and I must let go sometimes, too, and cast my lot with another of nature's imperfect but tenacious survivors.

Hold on, Donnie, hold on.

I'm often asked about Donnie. People want to know what happened to him. Is he OK?

Respecting his privacy, it's enough to say that Donnie did hold on. Graduated from college in horticulture, married, and runs a wholesale nursery business. Specializing in trees.

CLUCKY-LUCKY

"**H**ELP PREVENT TECTONIC PLATE MOVEMENT."
Message on the T-shirt worn by the man standing
beside me in line waiting for the Powell Street cable car in San
Francisco. A tourist. He's wearing the required silly shirt. His
wife's shirt says, "Hello, I'm an idiot from Wisconsin, Please Help
Me." This I could comprehend. But her husband's stand on tectonic plates was jabberwocky.

"OK," say I, "Tell me about your shirt."

Driving west from Wisconsin, he had tried to explain the landscape to his children. But they wouldn't buy the theory of tectonic
plate movement. No way was a huge chunk of the continent floating
around on lava and pushing up against the United States and making
volcanoes, earthquakes, and mountains as it slid under us. Dad was
hooted into silence by the children's razzberries of disbelief.

His wife discovered the T-shirt in a kitschy souvenir shop in
Reno. He wore it as a hair shirt of humility. The determined skep-
ticism of the young makes fierce and uncompromising adversaries.
His kids don't believe half of what he says, anyway.

He and I reflected on science and fatherhood. We concurred that it is the burdensome duty of adults to profess knowledge unconfirmed by direct experience. All that deep stuff you learn while growing up—you learn it, but you don't really believe it. We swapped examples:

For openers you're told how babies are made. Unbelievable. No way.

Almost as incredible as learning the earth will fall into the sun someday.

How about being told that algebra has a use in the real world outside school? Ha. And the Ice Age has to be a hoax. Half of North America covered with glaciers? A thousand feet of ice over Wisconsin? Never!

Split-brain theory is another lulu. Words in one half your head and music in another? Come on. And how about black holes in space? Quasars? And quarks?

Oh sure, you go around pretending that you are up to date on this theoretical stuff, but in your heart you know a lot of it must be dreamed up by scientists bent upon upsetting us civilians.

Based on personal experience, some of this ooh-wah information does compute. Combining several theories already mentioned, I am certain that the two halves of my brain have slid apart, leaving a black hole in the middle caused by the algebra quark. Believe it.

The all-time wonko idea is that birds are dinosaurs. Direct descendants right out of the Jurassic jungle. Oh, sure. However, fossil evidence of feathered dinosaurs really exists. And furthermore, I know of a fowl that is living proof of this hypothesis: Clucky-Lucky, the cannibal chicken of San Louis Obispo, California.

One Easter weekend, somebody's present of a baby chicken

got loose and wound up in the backyard of a pet-crazy family—friends of friends of mine. They raised her as Clucky-Lucky, the nomad chickette that grew up to be a substantial lady chicken of the Rhode Island variety. Cute. As chickens go.

But in her mature years Clucky-Lucky had grown unusually large for her breed and began to wander the neighborhood. She terrorized cats and ate their food. She assaulted dogs and chased people who annoyed her. When she began laying rancid-smelling eggs and began coming home in what was a distinctly inebriated condition, a veterinarian was consulted. Investigation proved the chicken had been eating cat food made out of *chicken parts*. And she was drinking beer out of traps set to kill slugs. Alas, Clucky-Lucky had become an alcoholic cannibal.

I have seen photographs of this chicken. Scaly legs with clawed feet. Razor sharp black beak. And yellow eyes that seem to shine with an ancient fierceness. Blow this bird up to the size of a water buffalo and you've got a dinosaur.

It's logical, too. If birds are dinosaurs, and chickens are birds, then chickens are dinosaurs. Or, if $B = D$ and $C = B$, then $C = D$. Finally, a use for algebra.

I explained all this to my colleague as we rattled along on the cable car. When he and his family dismounted, I heard his wife say as she walked away, "Not all the idiots are from Wisconsin." Never mind, lady, I know what I know. And I'll never turn my back on a chicken again.

PICKUP TRUCK

TRANSPORTATION IS MUCH THE TOPIC of the day. You've noticed. Our devotion to the car is worshipful. Guys, especially, will talk cars for hours. Eric Berne called it the cocktail-party pastime game: "General Motors."

Despite what you hear, it's not really a matter of economics. It's an image issue. In America, you are what you drive. Go out in the garage and look. There you are.

Well, my old hoopy has joined the cripples on the edge of the herd. And a new vehicle (image) is in order.

The silver-gray Mercedes convertible with glove-leather everything really felt like me. The bank did not really think it felt like me to them. The shiny black BMW motorcycle with sidecar kind of felt like me. My wife did not think it felt like her—especially the sidecar part. The Land Rover with gun rack and shooting top felt like me. But there are so few game-covered veldts around town now. The new VW Bug is *Consumer Reports*' choice, but a bug I am just not. If they had named it the VW Walrus or the VW Water Buffalo, I might go for it.

One of my former students suggested I put all my money into

drugs. Stay home and take all the trips I want. But that's not me—you don't bring back groceries from those trips. And nobody really envies you. And we must be envied.

It's clear that what would be fashionably hip is a fine piece of engineering—something that's luxurious yet practical, useful, and economical. Like a Porsche pickup truck that runs on Kleenex. Silver-gray, of course.

What I really want from transportation is not an image but a feeling.

I remember riding home on a summer's eve in the back of an ancient Ford pickup truck, with two eight-year-old cousins for company and my uncle Roscoe at the wheel. We'd been swimming and were sitting on inner tubes for comfort, and had a couple of old quilts and an elderly dog wrapped close for warmth. We were eating chocolate cookies and drinking sweet milk out of a Mason jar, and singing our lungs out with unending verses of "Ninety-nine Bottles of Beer on the Wall." With stars and moon and God above, and sweet dreams at the end of the journey home. And not a care in the world.

Now *that's* transportation. The way I like to travel. And that's me.

If you hear of a dealer, let me know.

DEAD END

THIS SHOULD BE CALLED "The Mystery of Twenty-fifth Avenue, Northeast." The story has semicosmic implications. It's about the fact that strange things happened where we once lived at the dead end of a dead-end street, two blocks long, at the bottom of a hill in north Seattle.

It wasn't much of a street to look at in the first place. I mean, it really didn't *call* to you to come down it. Kind of narrow and crooked and cluttered-up. Ed Weathers's van and his brother's GMC two-ton flatbed, and the Dillses' old Airstream trailer were just part of the vehicular obstacle course. Still, you could see all the way down from the intersection at Ninety-fifth to the end of it.

And there were two signs up there at Ninety-fifth, too—one on each side of the street. Big yellow and black signs. Both said the same thing: STREET ENDS. And down here at our end of the street was another sign, a big sign. Black and white, with stripes and reflectors and all. DEAD END is what it said. Right in the middle of the end of the street it said that. And you could see it for a long way off.

Well, for *all* that, people just drove on down the street anyway.

Not just part way, mind you. Not just to where the reality of the situation cleared up. No, sir. They drove all the way down, right up to the sign, the big black one with stripes, the one that said DEAD END.

And they read that sign two or three times. As if they were foreigners and had to translate the English. They looked on either side of the sign to see if there was a way around it. Sometimes they sat there for two or three minutes adjusting their minds. Then they backed up and tried turning around as close to the sign as possible. Backing and filling between our yard and Mrs. Paulski's marigold bed and the blackberry bushes across the street, running over some of each.

Funny thing is that once they got turned around, they never drove away slow and thoughtful—as if they'd learned something. No, they tore away at full throttle, as if fleeing evil. There was no pattern. All kinds of vehicles, all kinds of people, broad daylight and pitch dark. Even a police car a couple of times. And once a fire truck.

Innate skepticism or innate stupidity? I confess I do not know. A psychiatrist friend tells me it's a sample of an unconscious need to deny—that everyone wants the road or The Way to continue on instead of ending. So you drive as far as you can, even when you can clearly read the sign. You want to think you are exempt, that it doesn't apply to you. But it does.

Now I was wondering. If I had printed that up and then put little copies in a little box and attached it to the sign that said DEAD END, with a smaller note that said "Free Information Explaining Why You Are Here—Take One" . . . if I had done that, would people have read it? Would it have made any difference? Would they have been more careful of the lawn and the marigolds and the blackberry bushes? Would they have driven away any slower? I don't think so.

Perhaps I should have put up a sign at the top of the hill that said WAYSIDE SHRINE AT END OF STREET—COME ON DOWN AND CONFRONT THE ULTIMATE MEANING OF LIFE. IT'S A DEAD END!"

What effect would that have had on traffic?

Recently I went back to visit my old neighborhood after many years away.

The street is still a dead end. And not much else has changed. The neighbors say the unbelievers still drive all the way down to the sign, turn around, and flee. Life is still a dead end. And we still have a hard time believing it.

TESTING

I T'S BEEN REAL QUIET around our house this month. My wife is studying for her exams. Every seven years she must take and pass an all-day examination in order to be certified by the American Board of Family Practice Physicians as competent in her profession. She's liable for everything she's learned about medicine since the first day she walked into medical school.

As for me, I panic just knowing I have to renew my driver's license. I haven't taken an exam since college. Just being in the same house with someone who is studying for one gives my brain the worry-willies.

But it is a provocative notion—this business of being recertified every seven years. I wonder how it would be if all of us had to take a major exam as we passed through the decades of our lives after formal schooling was over. Suppose we had to prove our competency and proficiency as members of the human race. And if we didn't pass muster, we'd have to go back to class for retraining.

It makes some sense, actually. See, the only reason we're required to go to school is that we believe a nation is better off educated than ignorant. It works for the common good. But just because we got through the system doesn't mean anything really stuck or that we know how to apply what we know, does it?

Sometimes I'm appalled by my own ignorance. One of my favorite Peanuts cartoons has Lucy asking Charlie Brown, "Don't you wish you knew back then what you know now?" Charlie stares blank-eyed for a while, and then asks, "What do I know now?"

Think about it. What *do* you know now? Just what should we have nailed down cold in our brains by, say, age thirty, to justify our education and our continuing participation in life with people?

Reading, writing—still the basics. But right away there's trouble. Did you know that 22 percent of adult Americans are functionally illiterate? About forty million people would not pass reading and writing. It's true.

As for math—we should at least still be able to add and subtract and multiply and divide—even fractions. No algebra, though. If algebra is on the test, I'm going to get sent back to junior high school for the rest of my life.

What else? History's got to be on the exam. We get into continual peril because we lose track of the long and wide view of human experience. And basic civics has got to be tested. When only 38 percent of the eligible voters show up at the polls at a national election, some of us need reeducation about democracy.

By age thirty we ought to be clear on matters of money, sex, health, and love, because nothing causes more grief lifelong than our ignorance and ineptitude on these items.

So, basic economics and personal finance has to be on the exam—"Make a simple budget—demonstrate knowledge of balancing a checkbook." Ha. Right.

If you haven't got sex figured out by the time you're thirty, you'd better go back to class. Basic health—and first aid—should be current.

But love may have to be left off the exam. Most of us will never learn.

What else? How about knowledge of ethics, law, ecology, and science?

Sure, but all that is tidy-fact stuff. What about more subtle things? What should you know by thirty about art, music, and literature? How about friendship, honor, courage, truth, beauty, happiness, hope, imagination, wisdom, humor, and death? Whoa. This is getting out of hand. It seemed like a good idea when I began. I'm already over-questioned.

And we haven't even dealt with the existential items, such as:

Why is there Something instead of Nothing?

When will I have time, and who knows where the time goes?

How deep is the ocean—how high the sky?

When is enough enough?

What are people for?

Is there life *before* death?

Is it true that a little knowledge is a dangerous thing?

And if birds fly over the rainbow, why can't I?

BUFFALO TAVERN

ONE PORTION OF A MINISTER'S LOT concerns the dying and the dead. The hospital room, the mortuary, the funeral service, the cemetery. What I know of such things shapes my life elsewhere in particular ways. What I know of such things explains why I don't waste much life mowing grass or washing cars or raking leaves or making beds or shining shoes or washing dishes. It explains why I don't honk at people who are slow to move at green lights. And why I don't kill spiders. There isn't time or need for all this. What I know of cemeteries and such also explains why I sometimes visit the Buffalo Tavern.

The Buffalo Tavern is, in essence, mongrel America. Boiled down and stuffed into the Buffalo on a Saturday night, the fundamental elements achieve a critical mass around eleven. The catalyst is the favorite house band, the Dynamic Volcanic Logs. Eight freaks frozen in the amber vibes of the sixties. Playing stomp-hell rockabilly with enough fervor to heal the lame and the halt. Mongrel America comes to the Buffalo to drink beer, shoot pool, and dance. Above all, to dance. To shake their tails and stomp frogs and get rowdy and holler and sweat and *dance*. When it's Saturday night and the Logs are rocking and the crowd is rolling, there's no such thing as death.

One such night the Buffalo was invaded by a motorcycle club, trying hard to look like the Hell's Angels and doing pretty good at it, too. I don't think these people were in costume for a movie. And neither they nor their ladies smelled like soap and water were an important part of their lives on anything like a daily basis. Following along behind them was an Indian—an older man, with braids, beaded vest, army surplus pants, and tennis shoes. He was really ugly. Now I'm fairly resourceful with words, and I would give you a flashy description of this man's face if it would help, but there's no way around it—he was, in a word, ugly. So ugly he was beautiful. That kind of ugly.

He sat working on his Budweiser for a long time. When the Dynamic Logs ripped into a scream-out version of "Jailhouse Rock" he moved. Shuffled over to one of the motorcycle mommas and invited her to dance. Most ladies would have refused, but she was amused enough to shrug and get up.

Well, I'll not waste words. This ugly, shuffling Indian ruin could *dance. I* mean, he had the *moves.* Nothing wild, just effortless action, subtle rhythm, the cool of a master. He turned his partner every way but loose and made her look good at it. The floor slowly cleared for them. The band wound down and out, but the drummer held the beat. The motorcycle-club group rose up and shouted for the band to keep playing. The band kept playing. The Indian kept dancing. The motorcycle momma finally blew a gasket and collapsed in someone's lap. The Indian danced on alone. The crowd clapped up the beat. The Indian danced with a chair. The crowd went crazy. The band faded. The crowd cheered. The Indian held up his hands for silence as if to make a speech. Looking at the band and then the crowd, the Indian said, "Well, what the hell you waiting for? Let's DANCE."

The band and the crowd went off like a bomb. People were dancing all through the tables to the back of the room and behind the bar. People were dancing in the restrooms and around the pool tables. Dancing for themselves, for the Indian, for God and Mammon. Dancing in the face of hospital rooms, mortuaries, funeral services, and cemeteries. And for a while, nobody died.

"Well," said the Indian, "what the hell you waiting for? Let's dance."

GUMMY LUMP

WATCHED A MAN setting up a Valentine's Day display in a store window. It's the middle of January, but the merchants need to get a jump on love, I guess. Don't get me wrong—merchants are fine folks. They give us choices and keep us informed on the important holidays. How would you know it was Halloween or Valentine's Day or Mother's Day early enough to do something about it if merchants didn't stay on the job?

The other group I count on is kindergarten teachers. They always know about holidays, and when it comes to valentines and other evidence of love, no merchant can compete with them. What the kindergarten teachers set in motion, no merchant could sell—it's beyond price—you can't get it at the store.

What I'm talking about here is something I think of as the *gummy lump*. Once it was a shoebox, decorated and given to me by the oldest child. Then it became a repository of other relics of childhood given to me by the younger children. The shoebox became my treasure chest in time. Its components are standard: Three colors of construction paper—pink and red and white—faded now, aluminum foil, orange tissue paper, several paper doilies, three

116

kinds of macaroni, gumdrops, jelly beans, some little white hearts (the kind that taste like Tums) with words on them, and the whole thing held together with a whole big lot of white library paste, which also tastes like Tums.

Anyhow, this shoebox isn't looking too very good now. It's a little shriveled and kind of moldy where the jellybeans and gumdrops have run together. It's still sticky in places, and most of it is more beige than red and white. If you lift the lid, however, you will begin to know what makes me keep it. On folded and faded and fragile pieces of large-lined school paper, there are words: "Hi daddi" and "Hoppy valimtime" and "I lov you." A whole big lot of " I lov you." Glued to the bottom of the box are twenty-three X's and O's made out of macaroni. I've counted them more than once. Also scrawled in several places are the names of three children.

The treasures of King Tut are nothing in the face of this.

Have you got something around the house like a gummy lump? Evidence of love in its most uncomplicated and most trustworthy state? You may live a long, long time. You may receive gifts of great value and beauty. You may experience much love. But you will never believe in it quite as much as you believe in the gummy lump. It makes your world go round and the ride worth the trouble.

The three children are grown up now. They still love me, though it's harder sometimes to get direct evidence. And it's love that's complicated by age and knowledge and confusing values. Love, to be sure. But not simple. Not something you could put in a shoebox.

This sticky icon sits on a shelf at the top of my closet. Nobody else knows it's there. But I do. It is a talisman, a kind of cairn to memory, and I think about it every morning as I dress. Once in a while I take it down from the shelf and open it. It is something I

can touch and hold and believe in, especially when love gets diffi-
cult and there are no small arms around my neck anymore.

Oh, sure, this is the worst kind of simpleminded, heartrending
Daddy-drivel imaginable. I've probably embarrassed us both by
telling you. But its beats hell out of a mood ring or a mantra or a
rabbit's foot when it comes to comfort.

I have no apology. The gummy lump stands for my kind of
love. Bury it with me.

I want to take it with me as far as I go.

MOTHER TERESA

She died in 1997.

And this essay was written twenty years ago.

I removed it from the new manuscript, thinking the sentiments were shop-worn, the events out of date, and Mother Teresa a fading memory. So, you may well ask, why is the essay included here?

Seeing it in the reject pile troubled me. I read it several times again. And I realized the essay was not about Mother Teresa so much as it was about me and all those who try to resolve the inner conflict between self-interest and self-sacrifice. Trying to care about Me and care about Them and care about Us at the same time is an ongoing bewilderment.

THERE WAS A PERSON who profoundly disturbed my peace of mind for a long time. She didn't know me, but she went around minding my business. We had very little in common. She was

119

an old woman, an Albanian who grew up in Yugoslavia; she was a Roman Catholic nun who lived in poverty in India. I disagreed with her on fundamental issues of population control, the place of women in the world and in the church, and I was turned off by her naïve statements about "what God wants." People who claim to speak for God do more harm than good, if you ask me. She and her followers drove me crazy. They seemed so pious and self-righteous. I got upset every time I heard her name or read her words or saw her face. I didn't even want to talk about her. Who the hell did she think she was, anyhow?

However. In the studio where I used to work, there was a sink. Above the sink was a mirror. I stopped at this place several times each day to tidy up and look at myself in the mirror. Alongside the mirror was a photograph of the troublesome old woman. Each time I looked in the mirror at myself, I also looked at her face. In it I have seen more than I can tell; and from what I saw, I understood more than I can say. I could not get her out of my mind or life.

That photograph was taken in Oslo, Norway, on the tenth of December, in 1980. This is what happened there: The small, stooped woman in a faded blue and white sari and worn sandals received an award. From the hand of a king. An award funded from the will of the inventor of dynamite. In a great glittering hall of velvet and gold and crystal. Surrounded by the noble and famous in formal black-tie and elegant gowns. The rich, the powerful, the brilliant, the talented of the world in attendance. And there—at the center of it all—this little old lady in sari and sandals. Mother Teresa, of India. Servant of the poor and sick and dying. To her, the Nobel Peace Prize.

She was given the longest standing ovation in the history of the prize.

No president or king or general or scientist or pope or banker or merchant or cartel or oil company or ayatollah holds the key to as much power as she had. None is as rich. For hers was the invincible weapon against the evils of this earth: the caring heart. And hers were the everlasting riches of this life: the wealth of the compassionate spirit.

I would not do what she did or the way she did it. But her presence on the stage of the world dares me to explain just what the hell I *will* do, then, and *how*, and *when*.

Several years after she won the Nobel Prize, when I was attending a grand conference of quantum physicists and religious mystics at the Oberoi Towers Hotel in Bombay, I saw her in person. Standing by the door at the rear of the hall, I sensed a presence beside me. And there she was. Alone. This tiny woman had come to speak to the conference as its guest.

She strode to the rostrum and changed the agenda of the conference from intellectual inquiry to moral activism. She said, in a firm voice to the awed assembly: "We can do no great things; only small things with great love."

The contradictions of her life and faith were nothing compared to my own. And while I wrestle with frustration about the impotence of the individual, she went right on affecting the world. While I *wish* for more power and resources, she *used* her power and resources to do what she could do at the moment. Gandhi would have approved. He had some strange ways and habits of his own. But he did what he did.

Mother Teresa disturbed me and inspired me. And still does.

What did she have that I do not?

If ever there is truly peace on earth, goodwill to men, it will be because of women like Mother Teresa. In watching the millions of women marching in the streets of the world this winter, I was reminded that peace is not something you wish for; it's something you make, something you do, something you are, and something you give away! You begin with what you have, where you are, and pass it on.

Mother Teresa is dead now, of course.

Would you have wanted me to omit this essay because she's gone?

Or leave it out because I can't settle my own mind about Me and Them and Us?

That's the point, isn't it?

What she was, stood for, is not out of date or worn out.

It lives on as a challenge.

Not in her. In me. In you. In us.

CENSUS

THERE IS A clay tablet in the British Museum that's dated about 3800 B.C. It's Babylonian—a census report—a people count—to determine tax revenues. The Egyptians and the Romans conducted census counts. And there's William the Conqueror's famous Domesday Book, compiled in England in 1085. This need to know how many of us there are is old.

In our own country, the census dates from 1790. Counting people tells some interesting things. Especially since computers enable us to extrapolate trends into the future. Take this, for example: If the population of the earth were to increase at the present rate indefinitely, by A.D. 3530 the total mass of human flesh and blood would equal the mass of the earth; and by A.D. 6826, the total mass of human flesh and blood would equal the mass of the known universe.

It boggles the mind, doesn't it? That's a lot of meat.

Or consider this one: The total population of the earth at the time of Julius Caesar was 150 million. The population *increase* in two years on earth today is 150 million.

Or bring it down into a smaller chunk: In the time it takes you to read this, about 500 people will die and about 680 people will be born. That's about two minutes' worth of life and death.

The statisticians figure that about 70 billion people have been born so far. And as I said, there's no telling how many more there will be, but it looks like a lot. And yet—and here comes the statistic of statistics—with all the possibilities for variation among the sex cells produced by each person's parents, it seems quite certain that each one of the billions of human beings who has ever existed has been distinctly different from every other human being, and that this will continue for the indefinite future.

In other words, if you were to line up on one side of the earth every human being who ever lived or ever will live, and you took a good look at the whole motley crowd, you *wouldn't find anybody exactly like you.*

Now wait, there's more.

If you were to line up on the other side of the earth every *other* living thing that ever was or will be, you'd find that the creatures on the people side would be *more* like you than *anything* over on the other side.

Finally, this: There was a famous French criminologist named Emile Locard, and seventy years ago he came up with something called Locard's Exchange Principle. It says something to the effect that any person passing through a room will unknowingly deposit something there and take something away. Modern technology proves it. Dandruff, a hair, a fingerprint—things like that—remain.

Fulghum's Exchange Principle extends Locard's thinking: Every person passing through this life will unknowingly leave something and take something away. Most of this "something" cannot be seen or heard or numbered or scientifically detected or counted. It's what we leave in the minds of other people and what they leave in ours. Memory. The census doesn't count it. Nothing counts without it.

PASS IT ON

V. P. MENON was a significant political figure in India during its struggle for independence from Britain after World War II. He was the highest-ranking Indian in the viceregal establishment, and it was to him that Lord Mountbatten turned for the final drafting of the charter plan for independence. Unlike most of the leaders of the independence movement, Menon was a rarity—a self-made man. No degree from Oxford or Cambridge graced his office walls, and he had no caste or family ties to support his ambitions.

Eldest son of twelve children, he quit school at thirteen and worked as a laborer, coal miner, factory hand, merchant, and schoolteacher. He talked his way into a job as a clerk in the Indian administration, and his rise was meteoric—largely because of his integrity and brilliant skills in working with both Indian and British officials in a productive way. Both Nehru and Mountbatten mentioned his name with highest praise as one who made practical freedom possible for his country.

Two characteristics stood out as particularly memorable—a kind of aloof, impersonal efficiency, and a reputation for personal charity. His daughter explained the background of this latter trait after he died. When Menon arrived in Delhi to seek a job in government, all his possessions, including his money and ID, were stolen at the railroad station. He would have to return home on foot, defeated. In desperation he turned to an elderly Sikh, explained his troubles, and asked for a temporary loan of fifteen rupees to tide him over until he could get a job. The Sikh gave him the money. When Menon asked for his address so that he could repay the man, the Sikh said that Menon owed the debt to any stranger who came to him in need, as long as he lived. The help came from a stranger and was to be repaid to a stranger.

Menon never forgot that debt. Neither the gift of trust nor the fifteen rupees. His daughter said that the day before Menon died, a beggar came to the family home in Bangalore asking for help to buy new sandals, for his feet were covered with sores. Menon asked his daughter to take fifteen rupees out of his wallet to give to the man. It was Menon's last conscious act.

This story was told to me by a man whose name I do not know. He was standing beside me in the Bombay airport at the left-baggage counter. I had come to reclaim my bags and had no Indian currency left. The agent would not take a traveler's check, and I was uncertain about getting my luggage and making my plane. The man paid my claim-check fee—about eighty cents—and told me the story as a way of refusing my attempt to figure out how to repay him. His father had been Menon's assistant and had learned Menon's charitable ways and passed them on to his son. The son had continued the tradition of seeing himself in debt to strangers, whenever, however.

From a nameless Sikh to an Indian civil servant to his assistant to his son to me, a white foreigner in a moment of frustrating inconvenience. The gift was not large as money goes, and my need was not great, but the spirit of the gift is beyond price and leaves me blessed and in debt.

On several occasions when I have thought about the story of the Good Samaritan, I have wondered about the rest of the story. What effect did the charity have on the man who was robbed and beaten and taken care of by the Good Samaritan? Did he remember the cruelty of the robbers and shape his life with that memory? Or did he remember the nameless generosity of the Samaritan and shape his life with that debt? What did he pass on to the strangers in his life, those in need he met?

———————

Readers have passed on many variations of this story to me. Some are autobiographical—it happened to them. And some give credit to many different famous personages. What's true? Professional fact-checkers aren't sure.

But at least these three things are certain: Our belief in the necessity of the generosity at the heart of the story; our shared capacity to be part of the chain of generosity; and our belief in the enduring power of the simple compassionate gesture. We want these things to be true. And they are.

STARGAZING

WE HAVE BECOME catalog junkies. My sweet wife and I. Once you are on one list, you get them all. Especially in autumn they choke the mailbox, and we dutifully leaf through them by the fire after supper, amazed at all the neat stuff we don't have and never knew existed. It feels like the days of my childhood when the latest Sears Roebuck catalog showed up to fuel the flames of desire for more stuff.

My wife asked me what do I not have that I *really* want. I didn't tell her everything that came to mind, but once I set aside the more ludicrous notions involving lust, gluttony, and wanton greed, the discussion turned in a more meaningful direction:

I'd like to be able to see the world through somebody else's mind and eyes for just one day. To be inside and know what I know and see what they see and think.

There's a morning in the summer of 1984 I'd like to live over just as it was.

I'd like to speak a foreign language well enough to get the jokes.

I'd like to talk with Socrates, and watch Michelangelo sculpt *David*.

I'd like to be able to tap dance really well.

I'd like to see the world as it was a million years ago and a million years hence.

And so on and so forth. You get the drift of the conversation. We talked well into the night. And none of what we wanted could be had from catalogs. These were desires made out of nostalgia and imagination, packed in the boxes that dreams come out of.

Most of all, most of all, I'd like to have a living grandfather. Both of mine are mysteries to me. My father's father was shot to death in a saloon in Texas in 1919. In the same year, my mother's father walked out of the house one morning on his way to work and never came back. I still don't know why, and those who know don't say. In the fairy-tale factory in my mind, I imagine that if I had a grandfather, he'd be old and wise and truly grand. A bit of the philosopher, a bit of the magician, and something of a shaman.

If I had a grandfather he would have called me up and asked me if I had heard the news about the photograph of the latest solar system. Existing around a star twice as big and ten times as bright as our own sun—a star named Beta Pictoris. And around that star is a vast swarm of solid particles in a disk forty billion miles in diameter. And some of those particles are probably planets. All of it about fifty light-years from earth. Way, *way* out there. My grandfather would say I should come get him, and we'd go out and look at the stars and stay up all night and talk.

And I would go. We'd see Venus and Jupiter almost in conjunction with the bright star Lambda Sagittarii. The great winged horse of Pegasus riding high in the southwest sky. The misty patch of the Andromeda Galaxy almost overhead. And the Milky Way swung around since summer to run east and west. A shooting star would set my grandfather to talking about seeing Halley's Comet in 1910, and how that night of May 18–19 he witnessed what was probably the largest simultaneously shared event in human history. And how the world was divided between those who celebrated and those who watched in fear and trembling. My grandfather would make me promise to watch the return of Halley's Comet the next time around, on his behalf. And I would promise.

Along toward dawn we would talk of Orion, the Great Hunter, dominating the sky overhead. With the stars Betelgeuse and Bellatrix, the nebula in the belt, and Rigel and Saiph in the feet, pointing toward Sirius, the brightest star in the heavens. And we'd talk about how human beings have been looking at the very same stars and thinking the same things for so long. And how there must be life up there, same as here, and whatever it's like, it's looking at us. Do we shine? Are we part of some pattern in somebody else's night sky—a projection of their imaginations and wonderings? My grandfather would say he was sure it was so. My grandfather would say we're part of something incredibly wonderful—more marvelous than we imagine or can imagine. My grandfather would say we ought to go out and look at it once in a while so we don't lose our place in it. And then my grandfather would go to bed.

You'd like my grandfather. And he'd like you, I think. Happy Grandfather's Day to him, wherever he is. If you see him, let him take you out to see the stars.

And tell him I said I'd really like it if he came home for Christmas.

GRANDFATHER IN TRAINING

I'M A LITTLE UNCOMFORTABLE telling you about my grandfather. And you might be a little confused. I certainly am. After reading the preceding story, you might well wonder if the grandfather I'm talking about is real or not. What about the grandfather that died long ago and the one who disappeared? Who is this other one?

And I must answer that he both does and does not exist. It depends on what "real" is. I suppose it's harmless enough for a yearning to be so strong that what you need becomes very real in some corner of your heart. Picasso said, "Everything you can imagine is real." And I understand that. My *other* grandfather is made of that cloth of yearning and imagination.

In a sense we make up all our relatives, though. Fathers, mothers, brothers, sisters, and the rest. Especially if they are dead or distant. We take what we know, which isn't ever the whole story, and we add it to what we wish and need, and stitch it together into some kind of family quilt to wrap up in on our mental couch. I recently spoke separately with seven members of the same family about the same relative, and the stories did not agree. Memories

134

are creative. There is always the conflicting truth of many witnesses. Always.

We even make ourselves up, fusing what we are with what we wish into what we must become. I'm not sure why it must be so, but it is. It helps to know this. Here's the good part: Thinking about the grandfather I *wish I had* prepared me for the grandfather I *wish to be and am becoming*. It is a way of using what I am to shape the best that I might be. It is a preparation.

When I first wrote these grandfather stories, I was not a grandfather.

Now I am. Seven times over.

And the reality of my grandfather stories has shifted from the grandfather I wanted to have to the grandfather I have become.

I have lived my way into the truth of my stories.

GRANDFATHER

THE GRANDFATHER IN THIS STORY is the one I want to be. My grandfather called me up last Tuesday to ask me if I'd take him to a football game. Grandfather likes small-town high school football—and even better is the eight-man ball played by crossroads teams. Grandfather is a fan of amateurs and small scale. Some people are concerned about how it is that *good* things happen to *bad* people, and there are those concerned about how *bad* things happen to *good* people. But my grandfather is interested in those times when *miracles* happen to *ordinary* people. Here again, he likes small scale.

When a nothing team full of nothing kids from a nothing town rises up with nothing to lose against some up-market suburban outfit with new uniforms, and starts chunking Hail-Mary bombs from their own goal line, and their scrawny freshman tight end catches three in a row to win the game—well, it does your heart good. Miracles *do* happen.

"Murphy's Law does not always hold," says Grandfather. Every once in a while the fundamental laws of the universe seem to be momentarily suspended, and not only does everything go right, nothing seems to be able to keep it from going right. It's not always something as dramatic as the long bomb or the slam-dunk that wins ball games. There are smaller playing fields. For example:

Ever drop a glass in the sink when you're washing dishes and have it bounce nine times and not even chip? Ever come out after work to find your lights have been on all day and your battery's dead but you're parked on a hill and you let your old hoopy roll and it fires the first time you pop the clutch and off you roar with a high heart? Ever pull out that drawer in your desk that has a ten-year accumulation of junk in it—pull it too far and too fast—and just as it's about to vomit its contents all over the room, you get a knee under it and stagger back hopping on one foot doing a balancing act like the Great Zucchini and you don't lose it? A near-miss at an intersection; the glass of knocked-over milk that waltzes across the table but doesn't spill; the deposit that beat your rubber check to the bank because there was a holiday you forgot about; the lump in your breast that turned out to be benign; the heart attack that turned out to be gas; picking the right lane for once in a traffic jam; opening the door of your car with a coat hanger through the wing window on the first try. And on and on and on and on. You've got your own list.

When small miracles occur for ordinary people, day by ordinary day. When not only did the worst not happen, but you got the gift of what-could-never-happen-but-did. How grand to beat the odds for a change.

My grandfather says he blesses God each day when he takes himself off to bed having *eaten* and not having *been eaten* once again.

I know the prayer. "Now I lay me down to sleep. In the peace of amateurs, for whom so many blessings flow. I thank you, God, for what went right! Amen."

MARY'S DAD

I WONDER ABOUT JESUS'S MATERNAL GRANDFATHER. Mary's Dad. He's never mentioned, but he must have existed. Whatever your theological position, the Bible was peopled with human beings just like the rest of us.

Imagine.

Mary's Dad comes home from work one day. His wife and his teenage daughter are sitting at the kitchen table. His wife looks grim. The very air of the room feels heavy. Mary has her head in her arms, weeping. *Welcome home, Daddy.*

"So?"

"She's pregnant," moans the wife.

"So? Joseph, I suppose? They are betrothed, after all."

"Oh, no. That would be too easy. Your daughter doesn't do easy."

"Who, then?"

"She says . . . I swear to God she says . . . get this: 'An Angel of the Lord came to me in the night.' She claims a guy wearing feathers snuck into her room and did what he did."

"Right."

"Not only that, she says the baby's real father is God."

"Right."

"What do you mean, 'Right'—did you *hear* what I *said*?"

Actually, no. The father has not really been paying attention. This day-end crisis reporting happens all the time. He comes home tired from work. His wife and daughter are having a scene in the kitchen. She said this. She did that. I did not. Yes you did. Yadda, yadda, yadda.

Suddenly, the father's brain recognizes what his ears have heard. "WHAT THE HELL DID YOU SAY?"

It wasn't the last time he said that.

For years afterward it was the same. Jesus's maternal grandfather would come home from work. His wife would be waiting. "Well, Grandpa, guess what he did today, your grandson."

Water into wine, walking on water, loaves and fishes, healing here, healing there, and all the rest. Yadda, yadda, yadda.

It must have made it hard for the old man to sit quietly by while the rest of his friends bragged about their grandchildren. "That's nothing," he would say, "Wait until you hear this. You won't believe it." And they never did.

I can testify on this score. Nobody ever believes what a grandfather says about his grandchildren. Nobody even wants to know. And it must be even worse if you claim your grandson is the Anointed One and the Son of God, who walks on water.

Right.

MOTHS

A SUMMER'S EVENING. The front porch of Grandfather's farmhouse. By the light of an aged and sputtering lantern, I am playing a cutthroat game of Old Maid with five card sharks under the age of ten. Neighbors' kids and their friends. I am the "baby-sitter," from my point of view, and the latest "sucker" to play cards with them, as they see it.

We are eating popcorn laced with grape jelly, and knocking back straight shots of milk right out of the carton, which is being solemnly passed from hand to hand. We're all wearing cowboy hats and chewing on kitchen matches, picking our teeth. That's the rule—hats and toothpicks—you must look *serious* when you play cards.

And these are hard core bull-goose card whippers. I have been the Old Maid three times running, and am down to nine M&M's and four pennies in my pot. We are all cheating every chance we get. One of them has an extra deck and is passing cards under the table. I can't prove it, but that's what I think. Anyhow, what saved me from utter ruin at the hands of this criminal element were moths.

A flock of moths were corkscrewing around the Coleman

lantern. Every once in a while one would hit the hot spot and go *zzssshh* and spin out and crash like a fighter plane in a bad combat movie. Finally, one zerked out of orbit into the nearest spider's web, and the spider mugged, rolled, wrapped, and sucked the life-juice out of this poor moth so fast and so mercilessly it stopped the Old Maid game dead. A Green Beret ranger could learn something about the garrote from this eight-legged acrobat with the poison mouth.

The kids loved it. Encouraged by this homicidal scene, one of the boys leaves the table, rolls up a sheet of newspaper, and starts a king-hell massacre on the rest of the circling moths. Knocking them out of the air like a heavy hitter at batting practice, and then smashing them flat on the table, leaving little furry smudges and broken parts.

I leapt to the defense of the moths. It's bad enough that the lantern hypnotizes them into kamikaze runs and that spiders zap them into lunch meat, but small boys with newspapers are excessive handicaps to have to overcome.

"Why are you killing the poor moths?"

"Moths are *bad*," says he.

"Everybody knows *that*," shouts another.

"Sure, moths *eat* your clothes."

I could not sway them. They were convinced. *All* moths are *bad*. *All* butterflies are *good*. Period. Moths and butterflies are not the same thing. Moths sneak around in the dark munching your sweater and are ugly. Butterflies hang out with flowers in the daytime and are pretty. Never mind any facts or what silkworm moths are responsible for or what poisonous butterflies do. With a firmness that would have made John Calvin proud, moths were condemned, now and forevermore, amen. Out of the mouths of babes may come gems of wisdom, but also garbage.

That ended the Old Maid game. I stomped off, telling them I wouldn't play cards with killers, and they shouted they wouldn't play with someone who ate all the grape jelly while nobody was looking. I went to bed thinking if the future is in the hands of maniacs like these, we're in trouble.

The next morning the youngest kid came to me with a large dead moth in one hand and a magnifying glass in the other. "Look" says he, "this moth looks like a little teddy bear with wings and it has and feathers on its head."

"You like teddy bears?" I ask.

"Yes, I like teddy bears."

"You like small flying teddy bears with feathers on their head?"

"Yes," says he, "I think I do."

One must, sometimes at least, practice what one preacheth, and if one should look at moths without prejudice and with grace, one may be forced to reconsider small boys in a somewhat more generous light. Some moths can make silk. Some small boys can make sense. And know a tiny flying teddy bear when they see one.

NEAR-DEATH EXPERIENCE

IT IS SAID that people don't like to talk about death. Yet in just one afternoon I heard people say: "Your mother will kill you if you wear that outside the house." "Working overtime is murder." "I laughed so hard I thought I'd die." "My feet are killing me." And "Good luck—knock 'em dead."

Perhaps it's just that my mental monitor has been tuned to notice these phrases because a friend and I have been talking about near-death experiences.

He's a physician and aware of how well documented are the reports of those who believe they have died for a short time, crossed over into some other realm, and returned. Recently his own heart failed during surgery, and in the moments when he was being revived he had a classic near-death experience. Now he's deeply mystified by what happened and doesn't know what to make of it.

What is certain is the affect of the event. He's no longer afraid of death, for one thing. And he's living what most people would call a much higher quality of life—no longer so work-driven and in a hurry. He's moved from the fast lane to the slow lane of existence. His wife says a small dose of death improved his life.

Have you ever had a near-death experience? I have. Several times recently. Not quite the same as my physician friend. But powerful enough to get my attention and make me think hard about life.

This summer, driving through northern California, I noticed that a back door of my car was not completely closed. It took me about fifteen seconds to pull over to the side of the road, lean over into the back seat, and slam the door shut. As I drove on I rounded a curve to find that the driver of a small sports car had just shot through an intersection and hit an oncoming tractor-trailer truck so hard that he wedged his car underneath the truck, taking the top off the car and the driver. The impact jack-knifed the truck into my lane. If I had not stopped for a few seconds to close my car door, I would have been part of a deadly accident.

A week later, driving on across Nevada, I was a minute late on a curve where a huge tanker truck had lost its brakes, crossed my lane, and rolled over. If I hadn't taken time to wash my windshield at the last gas station, I'd have crashed into him head-on at death-dealing high speed.

I don't think I'm obsessing—just noticing anew what's always so close by.

I think of such things as I roll along in ease and comfort on a two-lane highway at 55 mph, passing hundreds of oncoming trucks and cars by about three feet—sometimes less. The slightest little twist of the wheel by me or them and my life is over.

Flying along at 37,000 feet in a jet, looking down at the landscape, I press my nose against what looks like a very thin sheet of scratched plastic. There's a little space and another very thin sheet of scratched plastic. After that there is only space—the air—whipping by at 500 mph at many degrees minus zero. If the plastic fails—it's the end of me—sucked into oblivion through a very small hole. Death by extrusion.

In my travels I've been to Gettysburg and Auschwitz and Hiroshima. I've stood in the very places where thousands died horrible deaths. Only the time frame was different. If I had been in the same place at that time I would be where they are now. Dead.

Awake in bed late last night, I watched the covers gently rise and fall as my sleeping wife breathed in and out. There was a slight pause at the top and bottom of the breathing. If it were not for the continuation of some unbelievably complex neuro-chemical reactions, each breath could be her last. I'm thinking that if her heart muscle does not squeeze again, our time together is finished. She breathed again. Alive. I considered waking her up to tell her all this. She'd kill me if I did.

Do I believe in near-death experiences? Yes.

Life *is* a near-death experience.

The leading cause of *death* is *life*.

Is there life after death? I'm dying to find out.

MUSHROOMS

THE FIRST TIME was at Aunt Violet's apartment near Embassy Row in Washington, D.C., the summer I turned thirteen. I had come by train all the way from Waco, Texas, to visit the Big City on the Potomac. Aunt Violet was a hard core social climber, a lovable eccentric, a heroine in an airplane crash, and an aspiring gourmet—and she thought my mother was a twit. All of which endeared Aunt Violet to me. Aunt Violet and I got along just fine. Until the night of the Big Dinner.

The lineup included a senator, a couple of generals, and assorted foreigners with their assorted ladies. A very large deal, indeed, for a kid from Waco who had been upholstered for the occasion by Aunt Violet with a striped seersucker suit and a bow tie. *Très chic!* Glorious me!

Anyhow. Having asked if I could help with dinner, I was handed a paper bag and told to wash the contents and slice them salad-thin. In the bag were mushrooms. Frilly-edged, mottled-brown, diseased-looking creepy things. Fungus.

Now I had seen mushrooms and knew where they grew. In dark slimy places in the cow barn and the chicken yard at home.

Once some grew out of a pair of tennis shoes I left in my gym locker over the summer. And fungus I knew because I had it between my toes from wearing the same tennis shoes every day for a year. But it had never occurred to me to *handle* mushrooms, much less wash and slice and *eat* them. *(My father told me Washington was a strange and wicked place, and now I understood what he meant.)* So I quietly put the whole bag down the trash chute, thinking it was a joke on the country-boy-come-to-the-city.

Guess they must have been *some* mushrooms, considering how old Aunty Violet carried on when she found out. To this day I'm convinced that's why she left me out of her will when she died. I had no class.

I confess that I still regard mushrooms and mushroom eaters with a good deal of suspicion. Oh, I've acquired the necessary veneer of pretentious sophistication all right—enough to eat the things when invited out to eat and to keep my opinions to myself, so I'm cool and all. But I still don't understand about mushrooms and mushroom eaters—not entirely, anyhow.

In fact, there are a whole lot of things I don't understand about entirely—some large, some small. I keep a list, and the list gets longer and longer as I get older and older. For example, here are a few mysteries I added this year:

Why are grocery carts made with one wheel that has a mind of its own and runs cockeyed to the other three?

Why do so many people close their eyes when they brush their teeth?

Why do people believe that pushing an elevator button several times will make the car come quicker?

Why can't we just spell it "orderves" and get it over with?

Why do people drop a letter in the mailbox and then open the lid again to see if it really went down?

Why are there zebras?

Why do people put milk cartons back into the fridge with just a tiny bit of milk left in the bottom?

Why aren't there any traditional Halloween carols?

Why does every tree seem to have one old stubborn leaf that just won't let go?

Is the recent marketing of cologne for dogs a sign of anything?

I know. Those aren't what you'd call industrial-strength mysteries. All the big-ticket things I don't understand are at the beginning of the list, and have been for a long time. Things like electricity and how homing pigeons do what they do and why you can't get to the end of rainbows. And even further up toward the beginning of the list of things I don't understand are the real big ones. Like why people laugh and what art is really for and why God doesn't fix some things or finish the job. And at the top of the list is why is there life, anyway, and how come I have to die?

Which brings me back to the subject of mushrooms. They were in this salad I was served for New Year's dinner, and I got to wondering about mushrooms again. So I got the encyclopedia out and read up on them a little. Fungi they are—the fruiting body, the sporophore of fungi. The dark underworld of living things—part of death, disease, decay, rot. Things that make their way in the world by feeding upon decaying matter. Yeast, smuts, mildews, molds, mushrooms—maybe one hundred thousand different kinds, maybe more, nobody knows for sure.

They're everywhere. In the soil, the air, in lakes, seas, river, rain, in food and clothing, inside you and me and everybody else—doing their thing. Without fungi there's no loaf of bread or jug of wine or even thou. Bread, wine, cheese, beer, good company, rare steaks, fine cigars—all moldy. "The fungi," says the big book, "are responsible for the disintegration of organic matter and the release into the soil or atmosphere of the carbon, oxygen, nitrogen, and phosphorus that would forever be locked up in dead plants and animals and all people as well." Fungi—midwives between death and life and death and life again and again and yet again.

There is a terrible and wondrous truth being worked out here. Namely, that all things live only if something else is cleared out of the path to make way. No death; no life. No exceptions. Things must come and go. People. Years. Ideas. Everything. The wheel turns and the old is cleared away as fodder for the new.

So. I picked at the mushrooms in that New Year's salad and ate them with respect if not enthusiasm. Wondering at what is going and coming. Quietly awed into silence by what I know but cannot always express. Borne by grace downstream into the great pool of The-Way-It-Is.

TERM LIMITS

"NOTICE: YOUR CITIZENSHIP HAS EXPIRED."
What? Yes! Term limits for citizens. Why not? This term-limits thing is still a good idea. If it is true that elected officials get corrupted if they stay in office too long, maybe it's the same for us who hold the political office of citizen. Let's at least set tough standards for all incumbents, citizens included.

Suppose that every twelve years our terms expired. Before we could requalify as citizens, our records in office would be judged. Remember, most of us got something for nothing the first time just by showing up here at birth. Now we have to qualify.

It's put up or shut up.

Let's use the same standards already set for any alien who wishes to become a citizen of the United States. As I write, in early 2003, the standards are being rewritten and raised, but in a nutshell, here are the basic qualifications:

First, you have to demonstrate competency in reading, writing, speaking, and understanding the English language.

Already a bunch of us are in trouble, ain't we?

The government also wants a recent photograph. Most of my friends are old, ugly and irritable. If looks count, they're out.

(I pause here, realizing I'm being both literal and sarcastic. I trust you can tell the difference. But having recently worked through the citizenship process with a by-marriage relative, I can tell you that many of the most disconcerting questions are taken from actual government documents.)

You have to pass a physical exam—no TB, HIV, STD or mental illness.

And all this qualifying costs money—application fees and lawyer fees and doctor fees and notary fees. Proving financial support is essential. Somebody must be able to support you. The government wants to be able to seize somebody's bank account for nonpayment of obligations. True. It seems that we no longer fling wide our doors to the tired, the poor, or the huddled masses.

Next, there are some "Additional Eligibility Factors."

Ever been a communist? A Nazi? A terrorist? Persecuted anyone because of race, religion, national origin, or political opinion? Ever failed to pay your taxes? Been a habitual drunkard? Advocated or participated in illegal gambling? Got a criminal record? If you answer yes to any of these questions, we don't want you. True.

Next, you must appear in person at the office of the INS and take written and oral tests to demonstrate your working knowledge of the history, principles, and form of government of the United States. I haven't taken the actual test, but here's the flavor of what might be asked:

Explain capitalism. Distinguish between the Democrats and Republicans. Define *liberal*. Define *conservative*. Did Betsy Ross really make the first flag? Who coined the slogan, "America—love it or leave it"? What rights are in the Bill of Rights? Whose rights are they? Is there a Bill of Responsibilities?

Add questions about current world affairs, local and state issues and economics. Name those who represent you in local and state government. Bad news. Most of us wouldn't pass without six more weeks in a high school civics class.

Finally, we're required to take an oath of allegiance in court. We must declare that we will support and defend the Constitution and laws of the United States of America against all enemies; fight if called on to fight, and work for the common good. Everybody—not just those who volunteer for military service.

What? I thought citizens in a democracy did or didn't do what they damned well pleased. It's a free country, right? Wrong.

About half the Americans I know wouldn't qualify for citizenship.

Besides not getting passing scores on the exam, some haven't participated in elections for a long time except to bark and bleed and moan a little louder just before the second Tuesday in November every year.

As for taking oaths, however, most of the people I know would swear to Almighty God that the problem with this country is all those lazy, stupid, double-talking, chowderheads who are running the government.

It's all the rage. "Term limits? Damn right! Throw the rascals out!"

But are we any better than the rascals we throw in? I say, let's find out.

I say: Tough standards for all elected and non-elected officials of government.

Suppose that every twelve years we lose our perks and privileges of office. We reapply, submit our record as citizens, get examined, tested, and checked out for competency, and pay our fees. If we pass, we get a citizen's license, stamped with big red letters saying: "USE IT OR LOSE IT."

If we flunk, we'll be given mercy and sent back for retraining in history, law, and civic responsibility. We'll be allowed two more chances to pass muster.

However. Recall our latest standards: Three strikes, and you're out.

CRAYOLAS

GOOD FRIENDS FINALLY PUT their resources together and made themselves a child. A son. Me, I'm the godfather in the deal. I take my job seriously.

So far I've introduced the kid to the good things in life—chocolate, beer, cigars, Beethoven, and dirty jokes. I don't think the kid cares much for Beethoven. But he's only a year and a half old. Which is why beer, cigars, and dirty jokes don't cut much ice with him, either. Yes on chocolate, though. I haven't told him about sex yet, but he's got some ideas of his own already. I won't go into details here, but if you have ever had a little kid or have ever been a little kid, then you know what I mean. We seem to figure out right away where certain parts are.

Also, I introduced him to crayons. Bought the Crayola beginner set—the short, fat, thick ones with training wheels. Every few weeks I would put one in his hand and show him how to make a mark with it. Mostly he just held it and stared at me. Then we went through the orifice-stuffing phase, where the Crayola went in his mouth and ears and nose. Finally, last week, I held his hand and made a big red mark with the Crayola on a sheet of newsprint. And *WHAM!* He got the picture. A light bulb went off in a new room in his head. *YES!* And he did it again on his own. And again. And again. Now, reports his mother, with a mixture of pleasure and pain, there is no stopping him from making his mark on the walls of his existence—wherever and whenever he feels like it.

Crayolas plus imagination (the ability to create images)—these make for happiness if you are a child. Amazing things, Crayolas. Some petroleum-based wax, some dye, a little binder—not much to them. Until you add the imagination. The Binney Company in Pennsylvania makes about two billion of these oleaginous sticks of pleasure every year and exports them to every country in the United Nations. Crayolas are one of the few things the human race has in common. That green-and-yellow box hasn't changed since 1937. In fact, the only change has been to rename the "flesh" color "peach." That's a sign of progress.

When I bought my godson his trainer set, I indulged myself. Bought my very own set of sixty-four. In the big four-section box with the sharpener built right in. Never had my own set before. Seems like I was always too young or too old to have one. While I was at it, I bought several sets. Got one for the kid's mother and father and explained it was theirs, not his. Fine gift.

What I notice is that every adult or child I give a new set of Crayolas to goes a little funny. The kids smile, get a glazed look on their faces, pour the crayons out, and just look at them for a while. Then they go to work on the nearest flat surface and will draw anything you ask, just name it. The adults always get the most wonderful kind of sheepish smile on their faces—a mixture of delight and nostalgia and silliness. And they immediately start telling you about all their experiences with Crayolas.

Their first box, using every color, breaking them, trying to get them in the box in order again, trying to use them in a bundle, putting them on hot things to see them melt, shaving them onto waxed paper and ironing them into stained glass windows, eating them, and on and on. If you want an interesting adult party sometime, combine cocktails and a fresh box of Crayolas for everybody.

When you think about it, for sheer bulk there's more art done with Crayolas than with anything else. There must be billions of sheets of paper in every country in the world, in billions of boxes and closets and attics and cupboards, covered with billions of pictures in crayon. The imagination of the human race poured out like a river in low and high places. Even presidents and prime ministers and generals all used Crayolas sometime in their lives.

Maybe we should develop a Crayola bomb as our next secret weapon. A happiness weapon. A Beauty Bomb. And every time a crisis developed, we would launch one first—before we tried anything else. It would explode high in the air—explode softly—and send thousands, millions, of little parachutes into the air. Floating down to earth—boxes of Crayolas. And we wouldn't go cheap, either—not little boxes of eight. Boxes of sixty-four, with the sharpener built right in. With silver and gold and copper, magenta and peach and lime, amber and umber and all the rest. And people would smile and get a little funny look on their faces and cover the world with imagination instead of death. A child who touched one wouldn't have his hand blown off.

Guess that sounds absurd, doesn't it? A bit dumb. Crazy and silly and weird.

Let me be clear about this. When I consider the horrible things we have developed at horrifying expense to drop out of the sky, and when I think about what those weapons will do—

well, then, I'm not confused about what's weird and crazy and absurd. And I'm not confused about the lack of, or the need for, imagination in low or high places. We *could* do better. We *must* do better.

There are far worse things to drop on people than Crayolas.

MIDWINTER

THESE NEXT TALES are about a real season as well as a season of my mind—midwinter—from about Thanksgiving to Valentine's Day. Midwinter has a lot of stress in it. Darkness, cold, family tension, hope, despair, religious beliefs wrapped in the confusion of social obligation and economic necessity. Christmas just happens to come in the middle of all this. Sometimes Christmas seems more like Halloween to me—all the ghosts and goblins that appear out of season.

The contradictions of midwinter drive me crazy. Some years I have wanted to hide in a hole, while in other years I wanted to organize extravaganzas, and some years I wanted to do both at the same time. One cannot live and be free of contradictions. Maybe I'll get used to that someday.

Several years ago I gave away my substantial collection of Christmas decorations, including many boxes of wind-up toys and a fine selection of wooden things made in Bavaria and Austria— the kind that go round and round driven by the heat from candles.

An era was over—pass the stuff on to the next generation—no fuss or muss in my house for Christmas. My kids stored these boxes in their basements and attics.

This year I missed my Christmas stuff. Took it all back. Put it all up. Had a fine time. Next, year? Who knows?

THE GREAT HEATHEN

"**J**ESUS WAS A JEW."

This is my father's voice. He's acting as a theological matador to my mother while she charged around the arena of our living room getting ready for the Christmas competition.

"Jesus was a Jew, dear. He wasn't a Christian, dear. And he wasn't born on December twenty-fifth, dear. Jesus is dead, dear. And he isn't coming back, dear. So calm down and shut up, dear."

My mother would retreat from the room crying, and my father would go back to reading his newspaper in peace, which is all he wanted in the first place. Peace on earth—beginning in our living room this evening.

He once asked me, "Son, do you know why God didn't have Jesus get married?"

"No, why?"

"Because having him crucified once was enough."

My father was a born-once-and-once-is-enough heathen.

My mother was a born-again-and-again-and-again supplicant of the Southern Baptist Church. There was a brick wall between them on the subject of religion—built and buttressed with bitterness over the years.

Every December I heard my father exclaim, "Jesus was a Jew, dear," and lay out his theological land mines. My mother would sob, "You're going to burn in Hell," and flee the room.

That's how I knew Christmas was coming.

Ding-a-ling ding ding.

In the late afternoon of a windy, cold December day—in front of the Woolworth's five-and-dime store in Waco, Texas, a middle-aged man in suit, tie, overcoat, and Stetson hat stands by a red steel tripod from which hangs a black iron soup kettle.

An eight-year-old kid, bundled up against the cold, stands beside the man. The kid is working up a little rhythm with a small brass bell. This is the first year the kid has been allowed to ring the bell. Warned by the man not to do anything silly, he is trying to mix joy with the necessary reverence required of one who has been entrusted with a serious job.

Ding-a-ling ding ding.

I am that kid. The man is my father.

For a couple of hours we are the Salvation Army.

My father was not a Christian. At least not by the standards of the Salvation Army, the Southern Baptist Church, or my mother. He was a heathen in their eyes and proud of it. So it was puzzling to me that the Great Heathen would work for the Salvation Army year after year as long as he lived. I never asked why. He never explained. But every year he was there.

Now I know the explanation lay in something he often said to me: "It doesn't matter what you say you believe—it only matters what you do."

After my father died his sister told me that their family home had burned down when they were children, leaving them destitute. The Salvation Army came to the rescue. My aunt said their family was so humiliated about their poverty and plight that they never talked about it. If it had not been for the Salvation Army, the family could not have stayed together. The Salvos practiced what they preached.

Now I understood why my father and I were there at the kettle every year.

Simple. We owed the pot. Do unto others . . .

The Great Heathen said I didn't have to be a Christian or a Jew to do right.

Ding-dang-ding-dang-ding-dang-dong!

HONG DUC

A SUNDAY AFTERNOON it was, some days before Christmas in 1979. With rain, with wind, with cold. Wintersgloom. Things-to-do list was long and growing like a persistent mold. Temper: short. Bio-index: negative. Horoscope reading suggested caution. And the Sunday paper suggested dollars, death, and destruction as the day's litany. O tidings of comfort and joy, fa la la la la!

This holy hour of Lordsdaybliss was jarred by a pounding at the door. Now what? Deep sigh. Opening it, resigned to accept whatever bad news lies in wait, I am nonplussed. A rather small person in a cheap Santa Claus mask, carrying a large brown paper bag outthrust: "TRICK OR TREAT!" Santa Mask shouts. What? "TRICK OR TREAT!" Santa Mask hoots again. Tongue-tied, I stare at this apparition. He shakes the bag at me, and dumbly I fish out my wallet and find a dollar to drop into the bag.

The mask is lifted, revealing an Asian kid with a ten-dollar grin taking up most of his face. "Wanta hear some caroling?" he asks, in singsong English.

I know him now. He belongs to a family settled into the neighborhood by the Quakers last year. Boat people. Vietnamese, I believe. Refugees. He stopped by at Halloween with his sisters and brothers, and I filled their bags. Hong Duc is his name—he's maybe eight. At Halloween he looked like a Wise Man, with a bathrobe on and a dishtowel around his head.

"Wanta hear some caroling?"

I nod, envisioning an octet of urchin refugees hiding in the bushes ready to join their leader in uplifted song. "Sure, where's the choir?"

"I'm it," says he.

And he launched forth with an up-tempo chorus of "Jingle Bells," at full lung power, followed by an equally enthusiastic rendering of what I swear sounded like "Hark, the Hairy Angels Sing." And finally, a soft-voiced, reverential singing of "Silent Night." Head back, eyes closed, from the bottom of his heart he poured out the last strains of "Sleep in heavenly peace" into the gathering night.

Wet-eyed, dumbstruck by his performance, I pulled a five-dollar bill out of my wallet and dropped that into the paper bag. In return he produced half a candy cane from his pocket and passed it solemnly to me. Flashing the ten-dollar grin, he turned and ran from the porch, shouted "GOD BLESS YOU" and "TRICK OR TREAT," and was gone.

Who was that masked kid?

Hong Duc, the one-man choir, delivering Christmas door to door.

I confess that I'm usually a little confused about Christmas. It never has made a lot of sense to me. Christmas is unreal. Ever since I got the word about Santa Claus, I've been a closet cynic at heart. Singing about riding in a one-horse open sleigh is ludicrous. I've never seen one, much less ridden in one. Never roasted chestnuts by an open fire. Wouldn't know how to if I had one, and I hear they're no big deal anyway. Wandering Wise Men raise my suspicions, and shepherds who spend their lives hanging about with sheep are a little strange. Never seen a flying angel, either, and my experience with virgins is really limited. The appearance of a newborn king doesn't interest me; I'd just as soon settle for some other president. Babies and reindeer stink. I've been around them both, and I know. The little town of Bethlehem is a war zone.

Singing about things I've never seen or done or wanted. Dreaming of a white Christmas I've never known. Christmas isn't very real. And yet, and yet . . . I'm too old to believe in it, and too young to give up on it. Too cynical to get into it, and too needy to stay out of it.

Trick or treat!

After I shut the door came near-hysteria—laughter and tears and that funny feeling you get when you know that once again Christmas has come to you. Right down the chimney of my midwinter hovel comes Saint Hong Duc. He is confused about the details, like me, but he is very clear about the spirit of the season. It's an excuse to let go and celebrate—to throw yourself into Holiday with all you have, wherever you are.

Where's the choir? "I'm it," says he. Where's Christmas? I ask myself. I'm it, comes the echo. I'm it. Head back, eyes closed, voice raised in whatever song I can muster the courage to sing.

God, it is said, once sent a child upon a starry night, that the world might know hope and joy. I am not sure that I quite believe that, or that I believe in all the baggage heaped upon that story during two thousand years. But I am sure that I believe in Hong Duc, the one-man Christmas choir, shouting "TRICK OR TREAT!" door to door. I don't know who or what sent him. But I know I am tricked through the whimsical mischief of fate into joining the choir that sings of joy and hope. Through a child, I have been treated to Christmas.

BRASS RULE

AND SPEAKING OF GIFTS, I should tell you a rule. It is not my rule, necessarily. It came from a very grumpy-looking man at a holiday office party. A man coming down with a full-blown case of Scrooge-itis. He had just unwrapped his dinky little present from under the office tree. In tones of amused sorrow he said to nobody in particular:

"You know, it's not true that what counts is the thought and not the gift. It just isn't true. My mother was pulling my leg on that one. I have collected so much gift-wrapped trash over the years from people who copped out and hurriedly bought a little plastic cheapie to give under the protective flag of good *thoughts*. I tell you, it *is* the gift that counts. Or rather, people who think good *thoughts* give good *gifts*. It ought to be a rule—the *Brass Rule of Gift Exchange*."

And he stomped off toward a garbage can carrying his little gift as if it were a dead roach.

Well, maybe so. It's a kind of harsh judgment, and cuts a little close for comfort. But the spirit of the season has been clear for a long time. God, who, it is said, started all this, cared enough to send the very best. On more than one occasion. And the Wise Men did not come bearing tacky knickknacks. Even old Santa, when he's making his list, is checking it twice. And the Angels came bringing Good News, which was not about a half-price sale.

To be honest, I do know what I want someone to give me for Christmas. I've known since I was forty years old. Wind-up mechanical toys that make noises and go round and round and do funny things. No batteries. Toys that need me to help them out from time to time. The old-fashioned painted tin ones I had as a child. That's what I want. Nobody believes me. It's what I want, I tell you.

Well, okay, that's close, but not quite exactly it. It's delight and simplicity that I want. Foolishness and fantasy and noise. Angels and miracles and wonder and innocence and magic. That's closer to what I want.

It's harder to talk about, but what I *really, really, really* want for Christmas is just this:

I want to be five years old again for an hour.

I want to laugh a lot and cry a lot.

I want to be picked up and rocked to sleep in someone's arms, and carried up to bed just one more time.

I know what I really want for Christmas: I want my childhood back.

Nobody is going to give me that. I might give at least the memory of it to myself if I try. I know it doesn't make sense, but since when is Christmas about sense, anyway? Christmas is about a child of long ago and far away, and Christmas is about the child of now. In you and me. Waiting behind the door of our hearts for something wonderful to happen. A child who is impractical, unrealistic, simpleminded, and vulnerable to joy. A child who does not need or want or understand gifts of socks or pot holders.

People who think good thoughts give good gifts. Period.

The Brass Rule is true.

CUCKOO CLOCK

Alwways wanted a cuckoo clock. A big, baroque German job with all kinds of carved foobaz and a little bird that leaps out once an hour and hollers an existential comment about life. So I got one. For my best friend, who also happens to be my wife and lives in the same house with me. See, the way this deal works is that she usually doesn't really like what I give her for Christmas anyway, and I usually end up with it in the end, so I figure I might as well start out by giving her something I want in the first place, so when I get it back I can be truly grateful. She gets the thought; I get the gift. I know it's wicked, but it's realistic and practical. *(And don't get high-minded about this, as if you would never think of doing such a thing. The hell you say. I've been around. I know what I know.)*

Anyway, I wanted an authentic antique cuckoo clock. But they cost a bundle. And this store had new ones—overstocked—a special cheap price—hot deal.

So I bought one. There were two messages written in small print on the carton, which I missed reading. "Made in South Korea" was one. And "Some Assembly Is Required" was the other.

The carton produced five plastic bags of miscellaneous parts. And an ersatz Bavarian alpine goatherd hut marked "genuine simulated wood." And to top it off, a plastic deer head that looked like Bambi's mother. I put it all together with no parts left over, thank you, and hung it on the wall. Pulled down the weights, pushed the pendulum, and stepped back. It ticked and tocked in a comforting kind of way. Never before had such an enterprise gone quite so well for me. The damned thing actually worked!

The hour struck. The little door opened. The little bird did not come out. But from deep in its little hole came a raspy, muffled "cukaa, cukaa, cukaa." Three cukaas? That's it? That's all? But the hands of the clock said noon.

I peered deep into the innards of the Bavarian alpine goatherd hut of simulated wood. There was the bird. Using an ice pick and a chopstick, I tried to pry the creature forth. It seemed loose. I re-set the clock to three. The clock ticked and tocked and then clanged. The door was flung open. No bird. Out of the darkness at the back of the hut came "cuck" but no "oo"—not even "aa."

Applying the principle of "if it won't move, force it," I re-sorted to a rubber mallet and a coat hanger, followed by a vigor-ous shaking. Reset the clock. Hour struck. Door opened. Silence.

Close inspection revealed a small corpse with a spring around its neck, lying on its side. Not many people have murdered a cuckoo-clock bird, but I had done it. I could see Christmas morn-ing: "Here, dear, a cuckoo clock. For you. The bird is dead."

And I did. I gave her the clock. And I told her the story. And she laughed. She kept the clock, too, dead bird and all, for a while.

The clock and its bird are long gone from our house now. And Christmas has come and gone many times as well. But the story gets told every year when we gather with friends in December. They laugh. And my wife looks at me and grins her grin and I grin back. She reminds me that the real cuckoo bird in the deal was not the critter inside the clock. I remember.

And me? Well, I still don't have a cuckoo clock of my own. But I have kept something. It is the memory of the Christmas message written on the packing carton. It said, "Some Assembly Is Required." To assemble the best that is within you and give it away. And to assemble with those you love to rekindle joy. Cuckoo to you, old bird, and Merry Christmas, wherever you are.

————————

When I retired from the parish ministry, my congregation gave me a parting gift: a first class cuckoo clock. Every time the bird came out, I thought of them—a bit cuckoo, but reliable. The clock fell off the wall in an earthquake two years ago. Smashed. Repaired. But somewhat unpredictable in the hours it keeps and the appearance of the bird. More like me, now, I suppose.

VALENTINE CHRISTMAS TREE

ALITTLE BACKGROUND: I often spend the winter in the mountains of far Southeastern Utah. San Juan County. Four Corners region. Not many people live around here. Mostly Navajo Indians and Mormon farmers. The national forest is large and nearby. So it's still possible to keep the old tradition of taking the family out to cut down a tree in the woods just before Christmas.

But times have changed here, too. The pockets of available fir and pine trees have diminished in size and number. The trees grow slowly—not as fast as the population grows. But another thing that's grown is the population's awareness of how people affect the environment, even in this remote location. The number of trees available for seasonal cutting has been noticeably reduced. The tension between nostalgia for the past and fear for the future exists even here. Many are shifting to having live or artificial trees. We understand why this is necessary, but we don't like it. It's depressing. Somehow, it just isn't Christmas without a real tree in the house.

In late December I drove a long way out into the back-country to hike for an afternoon in the winter sunshine. The area is high desert—sagebrush and scrub—but with red sandstone formations and sheltered side canyons that still contain pine trees. These evergreens are old growth remnants of the great forests, which dominated this landscape in wetter eras. Hiking up a streambed, I had what I thought was a hallucination. A fully decorated Christmas tree stood just ahead.

It was for real. A pine tree, about twelve feet high, gnarled and bent as it fought its way out of the rocks that had cradled its existence for perhaps two hundred years. Strings of popcorn and cranberries looped around its branches. Dried fruit and cookies and nuts hung from the branches like ornaments. And at the very top, perched a silver star with a tiny angel in the center.

It was the most beautiful Christmas tree I've ever seen.

Who did this? Two sets of tracks told me something—one large, one small—an adult and a child. These somebodies had come all the way out here, carried all this stuff, and carefully decorated the tree with things that birds and small animals might eat. More than that, they had the imagination to think of doing this in the first place. They must have had a wonderful time thinking through the logistics and then actually decorating the tree. And now they have a wonderful memory of one of the best Christmas trees ever. What's more, the tree lives on.

Later, now early February, I went back in the same direction looking for sunshine and solitude. I thought I'd check on the tree. But I had a hard time finding it. Because the same somebodies had come back and undecorated the tree. The fresh tracks in the muddy ground around the tree seemed to match those I had seen in the snow in December. All evidence of the decorating had been removed. And the star angel was gone. How did they get it up there and how did they get it down? A ladder? No. A child standing on a parent's shoulders would do it.

I'm inspired. My tree quandary is solved. I've picked my pine and enlisted two small co-conspirators. From now on, come December twenty-first, we'll decorate, and go back to undecorate on February fourteenth.

Imagine how the woods would look each December if more of us made a pilgrimage in the dead of winter to see the evergreen trees and decorate them with care? And then went back to restore the woods to their natural beauty. What would our children think?

As I said, this is a Valentine's story. It's about loving something—not just one's self or one's family or one's neighbor. It's about loving life—about loving this world—and seeing this world as our living room.

CHRISTMAS IN AUGUST

ONE YEAR I didn't receive many Christmas cards. One fetid
February afternoon this troublemaking realization actually
came to me out of the back room in my head that is the source of
useless information. Guess I needed some reason to really feel
crummy, so there it was. But I didn't say anything about it. I can
take it. I am tough. I won't complain when my cheap friends don't
even care enough to send me a stupid Christmas card. I can do
without tacky love. Right.

The following August, I was nesting in the attic, trying to es-
tablish some order in the mess, and found stacked in with the holiday decorations a whole box of unopened greeting cards from the
previous Christmas. I had tossed them into the box to open at
leisure, and then I ran out of leisure in the shambles of the usual
Christmas panic, so the cards got caught up in the bale-it-up-and-
stuff-it-in-the-attic-and-we'll straighten-it-out-next-year syndrome.

I hauled the box down, and on a hot summer day, middle of
August, mind you, in my bathing suit, sitting in a lawn chair on
my deck, with sunglasses, a quart of iced tea, and a puzzled frame
of mind, I began to open my Christmas cards. Just to help, I had

put a tape of Christmas carols on the portable stereo and cranked up the volume. Merry Christmas.

I opened the envelopes and set them out on the deck. Here it all was. Angels, snow, Wise Men, candles and pine boughs, horses and sleighs, the Holy Family, elves and Santa. Heavy messages about love and joy and peace and goodwill. If that wasn't enough, there were all those handwritten messages of affection from my cheap friends who had, in fact, come through for the holidays.

I cried. Seldom have I felt so bad and so good at the same time. So wonderfully rotten, elegantly sad, and melancholy and nostalgic and all. Bathos. Utter bathos.

As fate always seems to have it, I was discovered in this condition by a neighbor, who had been attracted to the scene by the sound of Christmas caroling. She laughed. I showed her the cards. She got weepy. I got weepy. And we had this outrageous Christmas ordeal right there on my deck in the middle of August, singing along with the Mormon Tabernacle Choir to the final mighty strains of "O Holy Night." "Faaallll on your kneeees, O heeeeeer the angel vooiiices."

What can I say? I guess wonder and awe and joy are always there in the attic of one's mind somewhere, and it doesn't take a lot to set it off. And much about Christmas *is* outrageous, whether it comes to you in December or late August.

BEETHOVEN'S NINTH

TALKING WITH A NICE LADY on the phone. She has a case of the midwinter spiritual rot. And a terminal cold she's had since September.

"Well," rasps she, "you don't ever get depressed, do you?"

"Listen. I get lows it takes extension ladders to get out of."

"So what do you do?" asks she. "I mean, what DO YOU DO?"

Nobody ever pinned me down quite like that before. They usually ask what I think *they* should do.

My solace is not religion or yoga or rum or even deep sleep. It's Beethoven. As in Ludwig van. He's my ace in the hole. I put his Ninth Symphony on the stereo, pull the earphones down tight, and lie down on the floor. The music comes on like the first day of Creation.

And I think about old Mr. B. He knew a whole lot about depression and unhappiness. He moved around from place to place trying to find the right place. His was a lousy love life, and he quarreled with his friends all the time. A rotten nephew worried him deeply—a nephew he really loved. Mr. B. wanted to be a virtuoso pianist. He wanted to sing well, too. But when still quite young, he began to lose his hearing. Which is usually bad news for pianists and singers. By 1818, when he was forty-eight, he was stone-cold deaf. Which makes it all the more amazing that he finished his great Ninth Symphony five years later. He never really *heard* it! He just *thought* it! Imagine that!

So I lie there with my earphones on, wondering if it ever could have felt to Beethoven like it sounds in my head. The crescendo rises, and my sternum starts to vibrate. And by the time the final kettledrum drowns out all those big F's, I'm on my feet, singing at the top of my lungs in gibberish German with the mighty choir, and jumping up and down as the legendary Fulghumowski directs the final awesome moments of the END OF THE WORLD AND THE COMING OF GOD AND ALL HIS ANGELS, HALLELUJAH! HALLELUJAH! WWHHOOOOOOOOM-KABOOM-BAM-BAAAAAA!!!

Uplifted, exalted, excited, affirmed, and overwhelmed am I! MANALIVE! Out of all that sorrow and trouble, out of all that frustration and disappointment, out of all that deep and permanent silence, came all that majesty—that outpouring of JOY and exaltation! He *defied* his fate with *jubilation*!

I cannot resist all that truth and beauty. I just can't manage to continue sitting around in my winter ash heap, wringing my hands and feeling sorry for myself, in the face of THAT MUSIC! Not only does it wipe out spiritual rot, it probably cures colds, too.

"So what's all this noise about winter and rain and bills and taxes?" says I to me. "So who *needs* all this talk about failure and confusion and frustration? What's all this noise about life and people being no damned good? Get up. Get on with it!"

In the midst of oatmeal days, I find within Beethoven's music an irresistible affirmation. In deep, spiritual winter, I find inside myself the sun of summer. And some day, some incredible December night when I am very rich, I am going to rent me a grand hall and a great choir and a mighty symphony orchestra, and stand on the podium and conduct the Ninth. And I will personally play the kettledrum part all the way through to the glorious end, while simultaneously singing along at the very top of my lungs. And in the awesome silence that follows, I will bless all-the-gods-that-be for Ludwig van Beethoven, for his Ninth, and his light.

I had the time of my life—MANALIVE!

———————

And yes, as a matter of magical fact, I did get to conduct that great piece of music—the Ode to Joy—with the Minneapolis Chamber Orchestra. Crazy dreams can come true when the dreamer has a crazy fairy godmother or two. The experience was all I hoped for. And a good deal more. It's too long to tell about here, but you can find my account of that improbable adventure in my book Maybe, Maybe Not.

SECRET ANNIVERSARIES — JANUARY

A MAN I KNOW keeps a bottle of vodka in his bathroom. Every morning as he begins his shaving routine, he takes the bottle out of the medicine cabinet and puts it on the glass shelf just below the mirror. As he lathers his face he considers himself in the mirror. And he contemplates the bottle of vodka.

He uses an old-fashioned straight-edged razor. As he shaves under his chin he considers how deadly dangerous the blade is, but he never cuts himself. When he has finished shaving, he replaces his razor and soap and the bottle in the medicine cabinet, and goes about his life.

The man's morning shaving routine has become a sacred ritual which exorcises demons and binds him to life as surely as if he had gone to his knees in prayer.

That bottle of vodka is half empty. There is a line drawn in indelible ink confirming the level—and the date the line was drawn. The top was screwed down tight on the bottle on the morning of that date. January 17. The bottle has never been opened since. There are little marks alongside the date—the kind used to indicate the passage of time: four straight lines with a slash across them to count five, plus four more equal nine. A slash will be made across those last four lines a few days from now marking ten.

Ten years ago, as he tilted the vodka bottle to his lips for the first of his frequent secret nips during the day, he saw in the mirror that the bathroom door behind him had opened a crack. The eyes of his only child met his. Those eyes were brimming with tears.

Time stood still. Nothing was said. The door softly closed. And the only eyes he had to look into were his own, reflected in the mirror. Bloodshot and puffy. In a jaundiced face veined and aged beyond his years. For the first time in a long time he really considered his image before him.

A stranger stared back. He was appalled. He wished he were dead.

Later that day he called a friend who was a member of Alcoholics Anonymous. That night he went to his first of many AA meetings and stood up to say, "My name is Ed, and I'm an alcoholic." When he got home he threw away all his hidden bottles of booze. Except one. As he screwed down the top on the bottle of vodka in the bathroom, he made a promise to himself: "Never again, so help me, God. Never."

This is a tough road to walk. It's never been easy. Many's the time he's locked the bathroom door behind him and considered taking just one more small drink and then replacing the missing alcohol with water to restore the level. He's even looked at the razor as a solution to more than the problem of needing a shave.

The memory of the face of his child at the door haunts him.

So. He has prevailed—keeping faith with his God, his friends, his wife, himself, and that child.

How I wish I could be there in the bathroom with him on January 17. Along with a brass band, gifts, family, and friends. Hurray! Thank God!

But anniversary occasions like these are usually solitary events, celebrated alone in the chapel of one's soul. It may be enough for my friend to draw that line marking ten years. And look up to face the man in the mirror with respect.

The good news is that there will be many such secret celebrations this month.

Many vows and resolutions are made in January. For all of us who don't live up to our best intentions, there are those who succeed. Their names will not be in the newspaper. No certificates, formal receptions, or parties will mark their success. But their numbers are greater than you may think. And they might be surprised at how many of the rest of us know about what they have done. The power of hope is confirmed by their triumph.

To all those who have kept their promises to themselves—who have managed to defeat destructive demons of many kinds, large and small—let it be known that the rest of us celebrate you. We think of you as heroes. Because of you we take heart for our own struggles.

Happy New Year!

Happy anniversary from us all. Press on.

HIGH SCHOOL REUNION

DESPITE SWEARING I would never do it, I went to the thirty-year reunion of my high school class, deep in the heart of Texas. I had not seen those "kids" since the night I graduated. And one quick glance confirmed my worst expectations. Bald heads, gray hair, double chins, wrinkles, fat, liver marks. Funny looking. Not funny.

Old. We're *old* now, thought I. So *soon*. And it's all downhill from here. Decay, rot, disease, an early grave. I felt tired. I began to walk slower, with a noticeable limp. I began to think about my will and make mental notes for my funeral.

This malaise lasted all of thirty seconds. Wiped out by the bright memory of two men I had met earlier in the summer at a truck stop in Burns, Oregon.

Mr. Fred Easter, sixty-eight, and his good friend, Mr. Leroy Hill, sixty-two. They were bicycling from Pismo Beach, California, to see the rodeo in Calgary, Alberta. They had been sitting on a bench by the beach, reading in the newspaper about the rodeo, and one of them said, "Let's go!" and they got up and went. And here they were in Burns in flashy riding suits, with high-tech bikes

189

and all. When I asked Mr. Easter how come, he laughed. "Why, just for the hell of it, son. Just for the bloody hell of it!"

Fifty-eight hundred miles later, via Colorado and the Grand Canyon, they expected to arrive home in October, unless, of course, other interesting things turn up along the way. They were not in a race.

I walked away from that encounter tall and straight and handsome and young—making new lists of all the things I would do and all the places I would go and all the things I would *be* in all the years ahead of me. Retire? Never! Die? Never!

As I write now, it's almost twenty years later. I've not forgotten Mr. Fred Easter and Mr. Leroy Hill. They would approve of what I've done in these twenty years. Next year—2004—my fiftieth high school reunion looms as a faint fuzzy marker in the onrushing future. Will I go? Probably not. Where will I be? Well, I've never been to that rodeo in Calgary. . . . Why the hell not?

SAN DIEGO ZOO

S AN DIEGO HAS A ZOO and a wild-animal park—the finest in the world, some say. Being a serious zoo fan, I once spent a day there. Zoos are great for adults—they take your mind off reality for a while.

For example, did you ever look real close at a giraffe? A giraffe is unreal. If there is a heaven and I go there *(don't bet heavy on either of those,* but *if),* then I'm going to ask about giraffes. Just what was on God's mind?

Little girl standing beside me at the zoo asked her mommy the question I had: "What's it for?" Mommy didn't know. Does the giraffe know what he's for? Or care? Or even think about his place in things? A giraffe has a black tongue twenty-seven inches long and no vocal cords. A giraffe has nothing to say. He just goes on giraffing.

Besides the giraffe, I saw a wombat, a duck-billed platypus, and an orangutan. Unreal. The orangutan looked just like my uncle Woody. Uncle Woody was pretty unreal, too. He belonged in a zoo. That's what his wife said. And that makes me wonder what it would be like if samples of *people* were also in zoos.

I was thinking about that last notion while watching the lions. A gentleman lion and six lady lions. Looks like a real nice life being in a zoo. The lions are so prolific that the zoo has had to place IUDs in each of the lionesses. So all the lions do is eat and sleep and scratch fleas and have sex without consequences. The zoo provides food, lodging, medical care, old-age security, and funeral expenses. Such a deal.

We humans make a big thing about our being the only thinking, reflective critter, and make proclamations like "the unexamined life is not worth living." But I look at the deal the giraffes and lions and wombats and duck-billed-what's-its have, and I think I could go for the unexamined life. If the zoo ever needs me, I'd give it a try. I certainly qualify as a one-of-a-kind endangered species. And examining my life sure gets to be a drag sometimes.

Imagine you and your kids passing by a large, comfy cage, all littered with cigar butts, cognac bottles, and T-bone steak bones—and there, snoozing in the sun, is old Fulghum with six beautiful ladies piled up around him. And your kid points and says, "What's it for?" And I'd yawn and open one eye and say, "Who cares?" Like I say, zoos tend to take your mind off reality.

The lion and the giraffe and the wombat and the rest do what they do and are what they are. And somehow manage to make it there in the cage, living the unexamined life. But to be human is to know and care and ask. To keep rattling the bars of the cage of existence hollering, "What's it for?" at the stones and stars, and making prisons and palaces out of the echoing answers. That's what we do and that's what we are. A zoo is a nice place to visit but I wouldn't want to live there.

NEXT SIX STORIES

The next six stories belong in a section by themselves. They are about a neighbor. The guy next door. When I think of all the places I have lived, what I remember most about why I liked living there was not the house itself. It was the neighbors—the great ones.

Most of us have had a good neighbor in our lives.

Or else we are that person to someone else.

We watch each other. And, for good or ill, learn from one another. The people next door play a substantial role in our lives. Yet we seldom choose them. I once went house-hunting with a friend who is a Native American. She was interested in the usual aspects of real estate—the location, the condition of the house, the price, and so on. But her two priorities were the neighbors and the trees. She looked carefully for a house with big, beautiful trees in the yard. And before she got serious about buying she went to meet and get acquainted with the neighbors. She said a house could be remodeled, even torn down and rebuilt. But fine trees take a

195

long time. And good neighbors make a huge difference in the quality of life. I agree.

As you will see in the stories that follow I had the good fortune of having a great neighbor. For the purpose of a good story, I have exaggerated a little—but not much. The facts are true. The guy next door was for real.

THE GUY NEXT DOOR

FOR SEVERAL YEARS I lived on a steep hillside in a decrepit summer cottage that had what a real estate agent called "charm." Which meant it was a shack with a view.

In keeping with the spirit of the house, I let the yard go "natural," letting what wanted to be there *be* there and take care of itself without any help from me. I remember announcing from the front porch to all living things in the yard: "You're all on your own. Good luck."

Up the hill above me lived Mr. Washington. In a sleek ranch-style-and-shingle dwelling with a yard kept like a combination golf course and arboretum. It was his pride and joy. An older man, insurance agent, and a mighty cooking champion when it came to barbecued ribs and brisket.

Mr. Washington was also Black.

And I am not. (I'm more putty-colored, actually.)

It was the late sixties, and I was an agitated activist, into civil rights, peace, and being obsessively liberal about anything you cared to mention. Mr. Washington was into—well, I'll use his *exact* words: "Fulghum, you are a downwardly mobile honky, and I am an upwardly mobile nigger, and don't you forget it!" Then he'd laugh and laugh. He looked down on me in more ways than one. And I looked up to him in more ways than one. An odd twist of sociology.

It made me nervous when he used the N word. I didn't mind "honky." It had a benevolent charm when he said it. But that *other* word—well. But that's what he called himself, and he always laughed when he said it.

Mr. Washington looked down from his porch onto my ratty residence with amused and tolerant contempt. He said he put up with me because I could cook better chili than he could and I had the best collection of power tools in the neighborhood.

Sometimes we played poker, and we both shared a fondness for fine cigars and the fact of wives who did not. We walked in the same marches of the times—the ones about racial justice and peace. And we liked the same music—jazz—once spending most of an evening comparing the solos of John Coltrane and Johnny Hodges.

Always there was his laughter—no matter how grim or serious the world might get, he saw the comic strip we were all in. He had the best laugh I ever heard.

In an uncommon way we provided a reference point for one another as we sorted out our daily lives, as you will see.

He's dead now. I really miss him.

I think about him when I cook barbecue—using his recipe for sauce. Mine's not as good as his. The secret ingredient was his laughter while he cooked.

DANDELIONS

MR. WASHINGTON WAS a hard core lawn freak. His yard and my yard blended together in an ambiguous fashion. Every year he was seized by a kind of herbicidal mania. He started fondling his weed-eater and mixing up vile potions in vats in his garage. It usually added up to trouble.

Sure enough, one morning I caught him over in my yard spraying dandelions.

"Didn't really think you'd mind," says he, righteously.

"Mind? MIND! You just killed my flowers," says I, with guarded contempt.

"Flowers?" he ripostes. "Those are weeds!" He points at my dandelions with utter disdain.

"Weeds," says I, "are plants growing where people don't want them. In other words," says I, "weeds are in the eye of the beholder. And as far as I am concerned, dandelions are NOT WEEDS—they are FLOWERS!"

"Horse manure," says he, and stomps off home to avoid any taint of lunacy.

Now I happen to like dandelions a lot. They cover my yard each spring with fine yellow flowers, with no help from me at all. They mind their business and I mind mine. The young leaves make a spicy salad. The flowers add fine flavor and elegant color to a classic light wine. Toast the roots, grind, and brew, and you have a palatable coffee. The tenderest shoots make a tonic tea. The dried mature leaves are high in iron, vitamins A and C, and make a good laxative. Bees favor dandelions, and the cooperative result is high-class honey.

Dandelions have been around for about thirty million years; there are fossils. The nearest relatives are lettuce and chicory. Formally classed as perennial herbs of the genus *Taraxacum* of the family *asteraceae*. The name comes from the French for "lion's tooth," *dent de lion*. Distributed all over Europe, Asia, and North America, they got there on their own. Resistant to disease, bugs, heat, cold, wind, rain, and human beings.

If dandelions were rare and fragile, people would knock themselves out to pay $24.95 a plant, raise them by hand in greenhouses, and form dandelion societies and all that. But they are everywhere and don't need us and kind of do what they please. So we call them "WEEDS" and murder them at every opportunity.

Well, I say they are *flowers*, by God, and pretty damn fine flowers at that. And I am *honored* to have them in my yard, where I *want* them. Besides, in addition to every other good thing about them, they are magic. When the flower turns to seed, you can blow them off the stem, and if you blow just right and all those little helicopters fly away, you get your wish. Magic. Or if you are a lover, they twine nicely into a wreath for your friend's hair.

I defy my neighbor to show me anything in his yard that compares with dandelions. And if all that isn't enough, consider this: Dandelions are free. Nobody ever complains about your picking them. You can have all you can carry away.

Some weed!

My delight in dandelions has generated a sizeable pile of mail over the years, including several sets of instructions and recipes for making dandelion wine. It was a common brew in the America of a hundred years ago, but the only place I know where it is commercially available now is in the Amana Colonies, in central Iowa, south and west of Cedar Rapids, but you have to go there to buy it.

However, it's not all that hard to make it yourself.

At the outset, a sound piece of advice from hard-won experience: If you're serious about making wine, consult the experts at your local retailer of brewery supplies to get an overview of the tools and techniques of home brewing. If you don't do this the first time you try to make wine, you'll do it the second time for sure. Believe me.

Here's a fine recipe for dandelion wine—makes about a gallon:

Get your equipment all set. Plan ahead. Consider, for example, how and where you can boil enough water to fill a six-gallon crock.

On a fine day in April or May, collect about six quarts of dandelion heads. You should not wash the flowers, which also means you should not collect them where pesticides or fertilizers have been used. Important.

Place the flowers in a clean six-gallon crock. Fill the crock with boiling water, cover the crock with cheese-cloth or muslin, and let the flowers steep overnight.

Next day, strain the mush through a colander to re-move the flowers, and then again through muslin to clear the liquid. Put the liquid back into the crock, add five sliced lemons, five sliced oranges, two pounds of dried yellow raisins, two cakes of brewer's yeast, and five pounds of raw sugar. Stir well.

Place the crock in a warm, draft-free place and cover it with a clean towel. Stir once a day for a week or until the brew stops bubbling. Skim off the scum every day, too. Let the sediments settle for a day or two.

Next, siphon off the wine into clean bottles. Corks or screw tops will both work. Place the bottles in a cool, dry place until December. You can drink it the first year, but it will also keep for several years and will im-prove over time.

Mark the bottles with the actual date the flowers were picked, along with a weather report. The ingredi-ents of the wine will thereby incorporate the memory of spring. The wine should have a clear, warm, yellow tinge—like a fine April or May day on which it was be-gun. Another hint from experience: open a bottle or two and taste before you give any away, just to make sure you got it right.

Winemaking is an art. You will have to make about

three batches until you get your skills to the point where the wine is consistently potable. But whatever the actual quality of the wine, you will have had a fine experience.

Some weed.

STICK-POLISHING

THE MAN NEXT DOOR cleaned his gutters yesterday. Downspouts too. He's done it before. I saw him last year. Amazing. I was forty years old before I even knew that people cleaned gutters and downspouts. And I haven't been able to get around to doing it once yet.

I live in awe of people who get those jobs done. The people who live orderly lives. The ones who always do what needs to be done and do it right. I know of people who actually balance their checkbooks each month. I know that's hardly credible, but I swear it's so.

These people also have filing cabinets *(not shoe boxes)* with neat, up-to-date, relevant files. They can find things around the house when they need them. There is order under their sinks, in their closets, and in the trunks of their cars. They actually change the filter on their furnace once a year. They put oil and grease on mechanical things. Their warranties runneth not out. Not only do their flashlights work, they actually *know* where the flashlights *are!* And they have extra batteries.

When their car was last serviced—they know that too. The

tools in their garage are on the pegboard—right where they are supposed to be. Their taxes are based on facts, not hunches and prayer. When they go to sleep at night, their list of Things to Do has a line through every item. And when they arise in the morning, their bathrobe is right there beside the bed and it is clean and new. Socks—right there in the drawer, folded into matching pairs. Yes! And as they prepare to walk out the door into a new day, they know exactly where their car keys are and are not worried about the state of the car battery or if there is enough gas to get to work.

There *are* such people. Ones who have it all together. Exempt from the reign of chaos and the laws of entropy. I see them every day all around me. Calm and easy pillars of society. They are the people in your high school yearbook you wanted to be. The ones who made it.

Well. I am not one of them. Out of the frying pan, into the spilled milk is more me. Most of the time daily life is a lot like an endless chore of chasing chickens in a large pen. Life as an air-raid drill. Never mind the details.

But I have a recurring fantasy that sees me through. It is my stick-polishing fantasy. One day a committee of elders will come to my door and tell me it is time to perform the ritual of the polished stick—a rite of passage for the good-at-heart-but-chronically-disorganized.

Here's the way it works. You get selected for this deal because you are such a fine person, and it is time you were let off the hook. First, a week of your life is given to you free of all obligations. Your calendar is wiped clean. No committee meetings, no overdue anything—bills, correspondence, or unanswered telephone calls. You are taken to a nice place, where it is all quiet and serene and Zen. You are cared for. Fed well. And often affirmed. Your task is simply this: to spend a week polishing a stick. They give you some sandpaper and lemon oil and rags. And, of course, the stick—a nice but ordinary piece of wood. All you have to do is polish it. As well as you can. Whenever you feel like it. That's it: *Polish the stick*.

At the end of the week the elders will return. They will gravely examine your work. They will praise you for your expertise, your sensitivity, and your spiritual insight. "No stick was ever polished quite like *this*!" they will exclaim. Your picture will appear on TV and in the papers. The story will say, "Man who is good at heart and well intentioned has thoroughly and completely and admirably polished his stick!" You will be escorted home in quiet triumph. Your family and neighbors will give you looks of respect. As you pass in the streets, people will smile knowingly and wave and give you a thumbs-up sign. You will have passed into another stage of being.

But more than that. From this time forward, you may ignore your gutters and downspouts. Your checkbook and files and forms and closets and drawers and taxes and even the trunk of your car will be taken care of for you. You are now exempt from these concerns. You are forever released from the bond of Things to Do. For you have *polished the stick*! Look at it hanging there over your mantel. Be proud, stick polisher! This is really something. And, it is enough.

Oh, don't I wish.

THE ODDS

I F YOU ASK my next-door neighbor what he does for a living, he will tell you that he is a professional gambler involved in organized crime. In truth, he is an insurance agent. He has a healthy disrespect for his business, and extends that skeptical mode into his philosophy of life. "We're *all* gamblers," says he, "every one of us. And life is a continual crapshoot and poker game and horse race." Then he adds, "And I *love* the game!"

He's a great believer in hedging his bets, however, protecting himself by betting both ways when the odds are close. Philosophically this gets expressed in these sayings mounted on his office wall:

Always trust your fellow man. And always cut the cards.

Always trust God. And always build your house on high ground.

Always love thy neighbor. And always pick a good neighborhood to live in.

The race is not always to the swift, or the battle to the strong, but you better bet that way.

Place your bet between turning the other cheek and enough-is-enough-already.

Place your bet between haste-makes-waste and he-who-hesitates-is-lost.

About winning: It isn't important. What really counts is how you play the game.

About losing: It isn't important. What really counts is how you play the game.

About playing the game: Play to win!

Does he really believe that? Does he live by it? I don't know. But I play poker with him. And I bought my insurance from him. I like his kind of odds.

WHERE THE SNOW GOES

MAN NEXT DOOR and I look upon one another with suspicion. He's a Raker and a Shoveler, as I see it. A troubler of the natural ways of the earth. Left over from the breed that conquered the wilderness. He thinks of me in simpler terms: lazy.

See, every week during the fall he's out raking little leaves into little piles. And every time it snows, he's out tormenting the white stuff with his shovel. Once, either out of eagerness or outrage, he even managed to shovel a heavy frost. "Can't let old Mother Nature get ahead of you," says he.

So I tell him he hasn't the sense God gave a stump. Leaves have been falling down for thousands and thousands of years, I tell him. And the earth did pretty well before rakes and people, I tell him. Old Mother Nature put the leaves where she wanted them and they made more earth. We need more earth, I tell him. We're running out of it, I tell him.

And snow—snow is not my enemy, I tell him. Snow is God's way of telling people to slow down and rest and stay in bed for a day. And besides, snow always solves itself. Mixes with the leaves to form more earth, I tell him. Think compost, says I.

His yard *does* look neat, I must admit—*if* neatness is important. And he didn't fall down getting to his car last snowtime, and I in fact did. And he is a good neighbor, even if he is a Raker and a Shoveler. I'm open-minded about this thing.

Still, my yard has an Oriental carpet of red and yellow and green and brown. And his doesn't. And I spent the same time he spent shoveling snow collecting it in bottles to mix with orange juice next July, and I taped the sound of it falling and then took the tape out of the cassette and used the tape to wrap around Christmas presents. *(Snow has lots of uses.)*

I gave him a bottle of vintage winter snow for Christmas, wrapped in some of that tape. He gave me a rake. We're giving each other lessons in the proper use of these tools. I think he's got no religion, and I'm trying to convert him. He thinks I've got too much, and he's trying to get me to back off.

But in the end, in the end, in the final end of it all—I win. For he and I—and even you—will become what the leaves and snow become, and go where the leaves and snow go—whether we rake or shovel or not.

Hair

HAIR GROWS AT the rate of about half an inch a month. I don't know where he got his facts, but my neighbor, Mr. Washington, came up with that one when we were comparing barbers. That means that about eight feet of hair had been cut off my head and face in the last sixteen years by my barber.

I hadn't thought much about it until I called to make my usual appointment and found that my barber had left to go into building maintenance. What? How could he *do* this? My barber. It felt like a death in the family. There was so much more to our relationship than sartorial statistics.

We started out as categories to each other: "barber" and "customer." Then we become "redneck ignorant barber" and "pinko egghead minister." Once a month we reviewed the world and our lives and explored our positions. We sparred over civil rights and Vietnam and a lot of elections. We became mirrors, confidants, confessors, therapists, and companions in an odd sort of way. We went through being thirty years old and then forty. We discussed and argued and joked, but always with a certain thoughtful deference.

After all, I *was* his customer. And he *was* standing there with a razor in his hand.

I found out that his dad was a country policeman, that he grew up poor in a tiny town and had prejudices about Indians. He found out that I had the same small-town roots and grew up with prejudices about Blacks. Our kids were the same ages, and we suffered through the same stages of parenthood together. We shared wife stories and children stories and car troubles and lawn problems. I found out he gave his day off to giving free haircuts to old men in nursing homes. He found out a few good things about me, too, I suppose.

I never saw him outside the barber shop, never met his wife or children, never sat in his home or ate a meal with him. Yet he became a terribly important fixture in my life. Perhaps a lot more important than if we had been next-door neighbors. The quality of our relationship was partly created by a peculiar distance. There's a real sense of loss in his leaving. I feel like not having my hair cut anymore, though eight feet of hair might seem strange.

Without realizing it, we fill important places in each other's lives. It's that way with the guy at the corner grocery, the mechanic at the local garage, the family doctor, teachers, neighbors, co-workers. Good people who are always "there," who can be relied upon in small, important ways. People who teach us, bless us, encourage us, support us, uplift us in the dailiness of life. We never tell them. I don't know why, but we don't.

And, of course, we fill that role ourselves. There are those who depend on us, watch us, learn from us, take from us. And we never know.

Don't sell yourself short.

You may never have proof of your importance, but you

are more important than you think. There are always those who couldn't do without you. The rub is that you don't always know who.

I recall an old Sufi story of a good man who was granted one wish by God. The man said he would like to go about doing good without knowing about it. God granted his wish. And then God decided that it was such a good idea, he would grant that wish to all human beings.

And so it has been to this day.

REFLECTION

EVER SINCE the first publication of *Kindergarten* I have been asked the same question by many readers: "So, didn't you learn anything *after* kindergarten?" The answer is, of course, yes. I learned what only time and experience teach. I found there are teachers who only appear later in life, when you have been made receptive by time and experience. My writing is the chronicle of the life I live. A keeping of accounts. Within an ever-growing list of what I've learned since age six, these sentences stick out:

Everything looks better at a distance.

If you made it up, you have to live it down.

Everything is compost.

There is no *they*—only *us*.

It's a mistake to believe everything you think.

You can get used to anything.

Sometimes things are just as bad as they seem.

It helps if you always have somebody to kiss goodnight.

Add those items to the Kindergarten Credo list.

There's more, but I'm not sure I can tell you. I'm often struck these days by what I know that I can't articulate. Somewhere beyond words there comes, at last, an understanding—a comprehension of the Big Picture—the unspeakable Unified Field Theory that even Einstein never got down on paper. Finally, I just get it.

Once I thought that getting the words just right was essential. Now I know the words will never be just right. A well-lived life is always under construction. I am no longer prone to argue with people about syntax and metaphors. What we have to say doesn't matter as much as what we have to do. Never mind the Credo—show the life. Don't tell me what you think or hope—show me your work. Get it? Do it.

Still, I am all too aware that I remain a living contradiction—a work in progress.

F. Scott Fitzgerald remarked that "Writers aren't exactly people . . . they're a whole lot of people trying to be one person." That's me. That's why the underlying theme in all my writing is *transformation*—a yearning for integrity so strong that it leads to the kind of change that alters one's life and the lives of others. I am trying very hard to live my way into the truth of my stories.

Finally, after wrestling with what I might have done differently if I had known then what I know now, I can give an answer when asked: "If you had your life to live over, what would you do?"

On careful reflection, all things considered, I would live my life over.

—Robert Fulghum, at age 65.

Coda

M Y FAVORITE BOOK ENDING IS not an ending. It's where James Joyce leaves off in *Finnegans Wake,* in mid-sentence, without punctuation or explanation. Some scholars believe the last phrase connects with the incomplete sentence that begins the book, implying an unending cycle. I hope it's so. I like that.

I have reconsidered, revised, and expanded this book as part of a cycle of rethinking about where I've been, where I am, and where I'm going. If all goes well, I will keep on doing that, and come back to Kindergarten again and

CONTENTS

To the Reader
From the Author   v

Credo   1

Deep Kindergarten   4

The Rest
of the Story   8

Spiders   11

Puddles   15

Haiho Lama   18

Angels   20

Hide and Seek   25

Chicken-fried Steak   28

Charles Boyer   32

Raccoons   34

Larry Walters   36

The Truth About
Larry Walters   38

Balloon Launch   40

Laundry   47

Medicine Cabinets   51

Jumper Cables and
the Good Samaritan   55

The Bad Samaritan   59

Bar Story   62

Help   65

Stuff   68

Vacuums   70

The Mermaid   73

Taxi   75

Summer Job   78

Weiser, Idaho   81

Bible Story   83

The Names
of Things   87

Water   90

THIRD AID	93		TERM LIMITS	152
YELLING	96		CRAYOLAS	159
DONNIE	98		MIDWINTER	163
CLUCKY-LUCKY	102		THE GREAT HEATHEN	165
PICKUP TRUCK	105		HONG DUC	168
DEAD END	107		BRASS RULE	172
TESTING	110		CUCKOO CLOCK	175
BUFFALO TAVERN	113		VALENTINE CHRISTMAS TREE	178
GUMMY LUMP	116		CHRISTMAS IN AUGUST	181
MOTHER TERESA	119		BEETHOVEN'S NINTH	183
CENSUS	123		SECRET ANNIVERSARIES— JANUARY	186
PASS IT ON	125		HIGH SCHOOL REUNION	189
STARGAZING	131		SAN DIEGO ZOO	191
GRANDFATHER IN TRAINING	134		NEXT SIX STORIES	195
GRANDFATHER	136		THE GUY NEXT DOOR	197
MARY'S DAD	138		DANDELIONS	199
MOTHS	140		STICK-POLISHING	204
NEAR-DEATH EXPERIENCE	145		THE ODDS	207
MUSHROOMS	148			

WHERE THE
SNOW GOES   209

HAIR   211

REFLECTION   217

CODA   219

ROBERT FULGHUM is a writer, philosopher, and public speaker, but he has also worked as a cowboy, a folksinger, an IBM salesman, a professional artist, a parish minister, a bartender, a teacher of drawing and painting, and a father. *All I Really Need to Know I Learned in Kindergarten* has inspired numerous theater pieces that have captivated audiences across the country. Fulghum is also the author of many *New York Times* bestsellers, including *It Was on Fire When I Lay Down on It*, *Uh-Oh*, and *Maybe (Maybe Not)*, as well as two plays: *All I Really Need to Know I Learned in Kindergarten* and *Uh-Oh, Here Comes Christmas*. He lives in Seattle, Washington.